Com

Regency Oaks

A Life Care Community Too Active to Retire!

(727) 252-0540 • (800) 965-2588

Special discounts on bulk quantities of this book are available to corporations, professional associations, libraries, and religious institutions. Contact:

DreamHouse Books, Inc.
1405 West 24th Street
Miami Beach, FL 33140
Tel: 305-534-2351
Fax: 305-534-2352
Web: DreamHouseBooks.com

Grandma Goes To Law School

Why It's Never Too Late To Live Your Dreams

Jeremy Goldstein
with Darice Bailer

DreamHouse Books, Inc.
Miami

DreamHouse Books, Inc.
1405 W. 24th Street
Miami Beach, FL 33140
Tel: 305-534-2351
Fax: 305-534-2352

Visit our website at www.DreamHouseBooks.com

Copyright © 2004 DreamHouse Books.

All rights reserved. This book, or parts thereof, may not be reproduced in any form without permission.

First Edition: May 2004

Grandma Goes to Law School: Why It's Never Too Late To Live Your Dreams

ISBN 1-883627-24-4

Printed in the United States of America.

This book is printed on acid-free paper.
Cover Design by George Foster

DreamHouse Books, Inc. is going to donate 7.5 percent of the pre-tax profits from the sales of Grandma Goes To Law School to help find cures for cancer and other charitable purposes.

Dedication

This book is dedicated to some very important people in my life. Foremost, my mother a woman of remarkable accomplishment. My wife Lisette who put up with all the late night writing and helped with the editing process. And my sister Darice Bailer, who is truly the accomplished writer of the family. With over two dozen books published by leading publishers such as Random House and Simon & Schuster, my sister Darice took my words and helped make everything more readable and enjoyable for you.

Finally, I would like to dedicate this book to everyone who regards aging as an opportunity to undertake new challenges.

The future is yours to enjoy!

About The Author

My name is Jeremy Goldstein and I am 41. You may ask, "What does a 41-year-old know about people over 50?" Well, I grew up with a lot of extraordinary older people who accomplished amazing things.

My parents and relatives were upbeat, whether they were 70, 80, or 90. They didn't think about age, and they carried on as if they were years younger. They didn't make excuses for themselves when they got older, and they held on to their youthful optimism. They were role models for their generation and mine. A day doesn't go by when I don't think about my relatives. I feel them with me all the time. I love the ones who are alive, and I loved the ones who unfortunately passed away.

I watched my father enjoy going to work and making sales calls into his late 70's. I remember him walking a little slower because of the arthritis in his knee, and I remember him taking a little nap in the car. But he always jumped up with the energy of a 20-year-old once we arrived at the customer's location. My father loved to help people, and he was constantly energized as a result. He underwent radiation and chemotherapy for cancer when he was 81, but the raging cancer never dimmed his hopes. My dad was eager to get better and get back to work, even on the day he died.

My mother is now 83. She's the inspiration for this book, because she just graduated from law school! You'll read about my mother and her remarkable journey to law school later on. The amazing thing is that my mother had already accomplished one feat at 70. That year, she earned a master's degree in social work! During her master's effort, I challenged my mother to get all A's. After all, she always had told me and my seven brothers and sisters to get all A's! Guess what? My mom did rise up to my challenge.

My mother's brother is Malcolm Glazer, the owner of the Tampa Bay Buccaneers. My Uncle Malcolm was 14 when his father died and he became the man of the house. At a young age, he took on the burden of supporting a family that included a set of twins, a 9-year-old brother and sister. He also went to work at the jewelry store his father had owned. There wasn't anybody else there to repair the watches and pay the bills.

Nobody ever gave my Uncle Malcolm anything.

He is a billionaire today, and he earned that money all on his own because he was never afraid to try new things and take on new challenges. I saw him build up an unbelievable number of businesses, one at a time. He went from the jewelry business to buying trailer parks, nursing homes, TV stations, and shopping centers. He bought stock in companies like Harley Davidson, Formica, Zapata, and Houlihan's. Now the owner of the Super Bowl champion Buccaneers, he is also an investor in the Manchester United Soccer Team in England.

My Uncle Malcolm is in his 70's today, and he still is on the hunt for good investments. He dynamically continues to challenge himself in new fields.

My mother's sister, Aunt Rosalind, first got me thinking about old age being a state of mind. She is 85 today, but I remember when she said "I don't feel 80" back at her 80th birthday party. To me, Rosalind doesn't look 85 either. She looks more like a person who drinks from the fountain of youth. My Aunt Rosalind just earned a Master Gardener degree from Cornell University to go along with her credentials as being a master judge and accredited landscape critic. She always finds a silver lining in everything. She rejoices in patting the soil around a new flower she plants out in her garden. She nurtures little seedlings ... and her soul.

My Uncle Jerome Glazer – one of those 9-year-old twins who lost his father back in 1944 – just celebrated his 70th birthday. Do you think he's sitting around playing shuffleboard? Hardly! Uncle Jerome is off *kayaking* in the ocean off the coast of Palm Beach! Most people would tell him he's crazy. Why, the waves could kill him! People don't know my Uncle Jerome, though. He's not afraid and doesn't care what others think. He just wants to have fun!

My Uncle Sidney Shapiro was always happy. He continued practicing law into his 80's. He stopped only when he was dying of prostate cancer. I remember talking to his co-workers at his funeral. They told me how much they were going to miss Uncle Sid. I do, too. He was always smiling.

What a family! And what a legacy to hand down to us in the next generation, and to the generation beyond ours!

Eugene Turula wasn't a relative, but he had an amazing spirit. Gene was an optical engineer who worked for me into his 80's. He had a job for life as far as I was concerned. Gene was one of the first people to show me that people can continue to contribute in their old age. The giving works both ways, too. While people like Gene are helping others, they are helping themselves. They feel a sense of accomplishment right to the end, even after others might have written them off.

Me? I've learned from all of these valuable role models, and I've tried to practice what they taught me. My relatives – from my mother to my aunts and uncles – taught me that many things others think are impossible really are possible. Just give them a try!

In the past twenty years, I too have become a successful businessman. In the ten years after my brother Julian and I purchased our company Navitar from my father, we were able to more than triple the sales. In 2004 alone, we expect to increase our business by more than 30 percent.

My mother inspired me to write this book. It is a tribute to her, and I hope that you like my effort. I want to show you that anything is possible for any one of us at any time. If you have the dream and you have the desire, it can happen. To help you achieve your dreams, here are some inspirational stories followed by a description of the seven characteristics these successful people share. Finally there's a step-by-step guide at the end of the book.

Jeremy Goldstein
If you have any comments or would like to reach me for any reason, you can contact me at the following address:

Jeremy Goldstein
C/O DreamHouse Books, Inc.
1405 West 24th Street
Miami Beach, FL 33140
Tel: 305-534-2351
Fax: 305-534-2352
Web: www.DreamHouseBooks.com

Grandma Goes To Law School

Why It's Never Too Late To Live Your Dreams

Inspirational Quotes
They said it before I did!

Youth is not a time of life: it is a state of mind; it is not a matter of rosy cheeks, red lips and supple knees: it is a matter of the will, a quality of the imagination, a vigor of the emotions; it is the freshness of the deep springs of life.

Youth means the temperamental predominance of courage over timidity of the appetite, for adventure over the love of ease. This often exists in a man of 60 more than a boy of 20. Nobody grows old merely by a number of years. We grow old by deserting our ideals.

Years may wrinkle the skin, but to give up enthusiasm wrinkles the soul. Worry, fear, self-distrust bows the heart and turns the spirit back to dust.

Whether 60 or 16, there is in every human being's heart the lure of wonder, the unfailing child-like appetite of what's next, and the joy of the game of living. In the center of your heart and my heart there is a wireless station, so long as it receives messages of beauty, hope, cheer, courage and power from men and from the Infinite, so long are you young.

When the aerials are down, and your spirit is covered with snows of cynicism and the ice of pessimism, then you are grown old, even at 20, but as long as your aerials are up, to catch the waves of optimism, there is hope you may die young at 80.
Samuel Ullman

*The road to success is steep, my dear.
The top of the goal is high.
Faith alone will bring you there.
Faith which cannot die.*
David Goldstein

If you can dream it, you can do it.
Walt Disney

Self doubt and fear of failure are the leg irons that keep us chained to the wailing wall of un-accomplishment.
Helen Hayes

Grandma Goes To Law School
"Why It's Never Too Late Too Live Your Dreams"

CONTENTS

Dedication	5
About The Author	7
Inspirational Quotes	14
Introduction	19
Grandma Goes To Law School	26
Why The Older We Get, The Easier It Is To Achieve Our Dreams: The Advantages Of Being Over 50	37
This Book Was Written For You!	44
Believe In Yourself With A Little Help From Family And Friends.	51
The Retirement Years: A Chance to Begin Anew	54
Margaret Hagerty, Champion Runner	60
Dr. Gail Fredericks, Unlikely M.D.	65
George Brunstad, English Channel Swimmer	73
Grandma Moses, Late-Blooming Artist	79
Ray Kroc, The Hamburger King	84
David Goldstein, My Beloved Dad	90
Reverend Dr. Hillary Gaston, The Lord's Servant	96
Mike Milken, Determined Philanthropist	104
Bunny Voss, A Reverend After A 40-Year Quest	110
Rosalind Klein, Master Gardener	116
The Million Dollar Man – The Ernie Harwell Story	121
Jack McKeon, World Series Winner	127
Seven Easy Rules For Success At 50 And Beyond	132
This Way To Your Dreams: A Step-By-Step Guide	141
Desire – The Secret Ingredient To Achieving All That You Want.	151
Exercise: The Body Is The Carrier Of The Mind.	154
Final Thoughts	156
Reference Section	157

Introduction:

In everyone's heart, there is always a dream – to lose 10 pounds. Write a book. Run a marathon. Finally earn that degree.

It's never too late to do any of these things.

Not even if you're 60, 70, 80 or 90.

You could be 120, too.

You can reach your goal and do whatever you want, whenever you want, health willing.

The people in this book did.

Take Jeanette Goldstein, for instance. Born in 1920, she always wanted to be a lawyer. But how many women from her generation even graduated from college, let alone law school?

Well, in the fall of 2000, at the age of 80, Jeanette started law school full-time at Syracuse University. She sat down next to the 22- and 23-year-olds, taking notes on constitutional law, civil procedures, and international relations. She had cataracts in her eyes, and she was starting to lose her hearing. A few Syracuse administrators encouraged her to attend school part-time, but Jeanette refused. She kept right on studying alongside young men with baseball caps turned backwards on their heads and free-spirited women with long hair and hip-hugger jeans.

At first, Jeanette's professors thought she was accompanying a grandchild to class ... until she came to class every day and sat in the front row during their lectures. Students shrugged and took a seat alongside her, hearing she was "smart as a whip." Though 10 percent of the first-year law school class dropped out, Jeanette hung in there. She graduated with her third-year Syracuse classmates in May 2004 earning a spot in the Guinness Book of World Records and the admiration of her professors.

"I have the highest regard for what she's undertaking at this stage in her life," says Frederick J. Micale, adjunct professor of law at Syracuse.

But Jeanette Goldstein isn't the only one of "The Greatest Generation" accomplishing something that is daunting even to the Generation-Xers who have yet to see a wrinkle or gray hair.

Take swimming the English Channel, for instance. American Airlines pilot George Brunstad flew across the Atlantic hundreds of times long after Charles Lindbergh completed his solo flight. But, George had never *swum* across the Channel. He trained to do that... at the age of 69.

Or what about running marathons? Margaret Hagerty smoked for nearly 50 years. Then, she quit and lit up the finish line of the New York City Marathon instead. She was 64.

As the men and women in this book reveal, you can dust off your dreams and accomplish and glean ... regardless of how many wrinkles you have.

Your only limits are the ones you place on yourself, according to Rev. Dr. Margaret "Bunny" Voss of Grand Rapids, Mich.

Rev. Voss believes that anything is possible at any time, although people often tell her they're too old to go after what they want. "Just think how old I'll be when I become a (doctor) (teacher) (lawyer)," they say.

Rev. Voss just looks at these people and asks, "Well how old will you be if you don't?"

In other words, they'll be the same age!

Chanel Hudson was one of Jeanette Goldstein's law school classmates at Syracuse. Chanel is a 24-year-old African-American from San Francisco who is the first in her family to graduate from college and attend law school. Watching a woman in her 80's be courageous enough to take the same course load as her makes Chanel realize that there's no excuse for anyone not to get an education.

And, she said that Jeanette "just motivates me to keep striving to go after what I originally came here for."

Still, older people have been accomplishing amazing things for ages.

In Alex Comfort's book, A Good Age, there are illustrations of famous septuagenarians and octogenarians throughout history.

Ben Franklin was 70 when he helped signed the Declaration of Independence - a historic document he helped write.

Michaelangelo became chief architect of St. Peter's in Rome at the age of 71.

Claude Monet - the Impressionist master - painted water lilies on canvas at 73.

French poet, playwright and novelist Victor Hugo published his last masterpiece at 81.

Duncan MacLean won a silver medal at the 1975 World Veterans' Olympics ... at 90.

What did all these famous people have that you have?

Desire...because if you didn't have that burning desire inside you, you wouldn't be reading this book!

Perhaps one of these stories will inspire you to go back to school, come out of retirement, write your novel, or start your own business.

Perhaps the stories and the unifying principles in this book will give you the motivation to start a new career.

Whether you are in your 20's, 50's or 90's, it is not too late to achieve what you want. It is not too late to face up to the things you may have put off in order to do what you thought was important at the time. You'll feel better reconciling your inner feelings, too. Our inner psyches never forget our dreams, and those dreams continue to gnaw away at us until they are fulfilled.

It is not easy to take a first step in the direction of a goal, or to change course and wade in unfamiliar waters the way Jeanette Goldstein did in law school. But, it is not impossible either. What makes it possible is desire. This "desire" will help you keep going even when you wish you had more support from your family and friends. And, that support will come once you start working toward your goals. Friends will jump on your bandwagon like fans on a winning team!

Yet it is not easy to give up a secure salary for a not-so-secure future. When Reverend Dr. Hillary Gaston, Sr. cut his pay in half to minister to his people, his wife eventually left him. Rev. Gaston had to make sacrifices with his pay cut, and his wife was one of them. She had a difficult time accepting her downsizing. And, the more anyone makes, the harder it is to let go. Sometimes it's easier to make a move when we aren't quite as well-off. There is less to lose financially.

Lucky for all of us, we are living longer. And, this book is full of stories of people who did not achieve their dreams until much later on in life.

Dr. Gail Fredericks is another example of someone who changed professions after years of dreaming about it. Dr. Fredericks wanted to become a medical doctor, and she did at age 51.

Maybe this book will help you live out your dream by showing you people like Dr. Gail who did just that. And, in a later chapter, you will discover the seven common characteristics the people in this book all shared. The men and women interviewed for this book, you see, were all positive thinkers who expected success and were philosophical when they didn't achieve it. They bounced back quickly from disappointment and moved on. If you study these seven common characteristics and adopt them in your own life, you will be on your way to realizing your dream.

And if you're under 50, you still can embrace the principles found in this book, because if you do, you'll be blessed with the happiness that comes from doing just what you always wanted to do.

Just start with a few words of advice. As Rev. Voss says, "Get your butt in gear and go!"

Or, as Rosalind Klein puts it, *"Get off your duff!"*

Chapter One
Grandma Goes To Law School

(Note: Pride leads me to present this as the first chapter of this book. I'll get back to philosophy later, but only after proudly honoring someone whose accomplishment is not only extraordinary ... it's personally significant for me. JG)

When the Honorable Elijah Huling, Jr. first saw the 82-year-old woman walking into his medical malpractice class at Syracuse University, he thought she was a parent. It never crossed the judge's mind that Jeanette Goldstein might be one of his students.
But she was.
"I was shocked," the visiting law professor said.
Judge Huling's next reaction was that Jeanette must be a part-time student at the College of Law.
But she wasn't.
And so Judge Huling chuckled, recalling that first introduction in an interview at school. "Amazing," he said. In fact, the Baldwinsville, N.Y., judge says Jeanette Goldstein was one of the most remarkable students he has ever had as a visiting professor at Syracuse University's College of Law. She was, in fact, so remarkable that Judge Huling went home to

have a heart-to-heart talk with his children after he met her. His children spent about a half hour per week-night on their homework, and Judge Huling scolded them.

You'd better spend a little more time on your studies because I have an 80-year-old student who's working a lot harder than you!

Jeanette really did work hard.

Her determined motto: Be prepared.

Judge Huling, like all Jeanette's Syracuse law professors, said Jeanette was always prepared for class. She studied hard for one of Judge Huling's exams and refused to sign a petition against him after classmates decided the test was unfairly difficult.

Jeanette just stared at the grade next to her assigned student number after grades were posted. She had cataracts and thought she was reading the grade wrong. That couldn't be a B next to her name, could it?

Jeanette asked Judge Huling to check the grade. "Is that mine?" she asked.

Yes, it was. Jeanette had scored one of the highest grades on an exam that most of her classmates thought had been one of the most difficult of their law school careers. Other students would be pleased just to pass, but Jeanette wanted a good grade.

"I'm amazed," said Judge Huling, smiling during his interview. "The competition is intense and cut-throat here, and she's sticking herself right in that competition. She is in the pool, swimming with all the rest of the sharks. It takes courage to do that. I know the environment, and to step out of a familiar environment takes a lot of courage. Courage and fortitude. She just gets in there and plugs away."

Judge Huling didn't know that going to law school had been my mother's dream.

As long as I can remember, my mother wanted to be a lawyer. In fact, she has had this desire since 1955 when she flew to Japan with my father, David Goldstein, on a business trip. My father's company made movie camera lenses, and my father was always looking for new optical products to sell. In 1955, my father signed a contract with Olympus Corporation of Japan to be the exclusive U.S. importer of their microscopes. My mother enjoyed sitting in on the contract negotiations. In fact, she came to feel she could do a better job than the lawyers.

Could she be a lawyer? My mother had five young children at the time and lived in Rochester, N.Y. She had someone to help her with the children, but still... where could she even go to law school? Rochester didn't have one.

Forty-one years later, my father died and my mother was grief-stricken. Like so many widows, she'd lost the man she'd loved for over 50 years and didn't know what to do with herself. Then she thought of her old dream, becoming a lawyer. "Better late than never," she said.

But, what would we – her children – think? There were eight of us now, all of us grown adults. "I didn't consider other people's reactions so much as considering my children's reactions," my mother said. "And what surprised me is that even though I was convinced everyone would think I was crazy, they all supported me and thought it was a great idea!"

Here comes the student.

My mother got up the nerve to take the LSAT and apply to two law schools – Nova Southeastern University in Ft. Lauderdale, Florida, and Syracuse University in Syracuse, New York. To her surprise, both schools accepted her! My mother chose Syracuse because of its convenience – a little over an hour away from where she lived in Rochester.

Margery Connor, a former associate dean for student affairs at the College of Law who retired while my mother was a third-year student there, said that the school accepted her because her LSAT scores and her graduate school grades were good. "I looked at her resume," Ms. Connor said. "Her numbers were enough to let her in."

The school couldn't discriminate against Jeanette because of her age. Besides, Ms. Connor said, "I really advocate for the non-traditional student."

Ms. Connor knew that Jeanette's age might actually benefit both students and faculty. "She had a point of view that she could share with people," Ms. Connor said. It would come from her age.

"She is most special because she has had not only life experiences but she's had business experiences too," said Professor Frederick J. Micale, an adjunct professor. "She brings that to class and makes a real contribution. I think it's not only something I appreciate, but other students do, too."

Professor Micale said students respect the courage of someone Jeanette's age to undertake the rigors of law. Syracuse had students from all over the world, and some had language and cultural barriers.

In Jeanette's case, the barriers were physical, Professor Micale pointed out. Jeanette's eyes and ears were starting to fail. She sat attentively in the front row of the lecture hall because she couldn't see the board or screen if she sat any farther back. On the negative side, while sitting in front she couldn't hear the students in the rear.

Administrators wondered if she had the stamina to stick it out.

"She drew a lot of attention and people had doubts," Ms. Connor said. "Law school is rigorous.

You don't get a lot of rest. I was worried about her capacity to do it all."

Ms. Connor suggested that Jeanette enroll part-time.

Jeanette refused.

So, in the fall of 2000, Jeanette sat down beside students in their 20's and started scribbling away on that legal pad. She was the mother of eight children and the grandmother of 22. That was about the age of most of her classmates, too. There were a few doctors, engineers or social workers in their 50's, and a retired nun had once taken courses at the law school. But Jeanette was the oldest. And, while most of the younger students clicked away on their laptops in class, Jeanette took notes in script. She couldn't type or use a computer.

Students set their water bottles down and sat next to her, amazed at her initiative. "Everybody was talking about this 80-year-old," said Jason Cleckner, a 23-year-old classmate who sat next to Jeanette in Civil Procedures class.

"Was there really a president named Ronald Reagan?"

Professors were dumbfounded that they actually had a student in class who had lived through Watergate or the Reagan and Carter eras, ancient events and presidents to these students who were born years after. Jeanette could nod her head when professors spoke of the Great Depression, too. She had lived through it.

"I can make a lot of references to something that happened quite a while ago," said Professor Christian C. Day.

Whatever grades she earned in any of her classes were hers. Professors did not help her out. That's because each student was assigned a number, and the number was all the professors ever saw on exams or papers – without ever knowing whose it was. Although Jeanette couldn't type exams on a computer in class, the school assigned her a typist who sat beside her. Thus, all her work was evaluated without her professors ever knowing that it was hers.

The instructors, moreover, graded on a bell curve. Very few students received As, and a few did receive Ds and Fs. My mother passed all her courses and survived, while a small percentage of students were not performing up to expectation and were asked to leave.

To be honest, it wasn't easy for my mother that first year either. She had a master's degree in social work. But, she said, "social work was a breeze in comparison to law school."

Maybe it was because my mother had been out of school for so many years. "The students coming directly out of college, they knew the shortcuts," my mother said. "They knew aspects to get through the course much easier than I did."

Nevertheless, she persevered that first year, even pulling all-nighters when she needed to.

Ms. Connor admitted that my mother had a rocky time. "The first year is the hardest. But she managed to get through it."

After that first year, my mother started recommending classes to the students who were a year or two behind her.

"She was right on target, too," said Chanel Hudson, 24, of San Francisco.

As the semesters passed and graduation neared, my mother's confidence and physical strength grew. Each day, she was forced to take a brisk walk. She'd walk from her graduate student dormitory to the bus stop, and from the bus to the law school. Then, there was the return trip at night. The wind was often blowing and it seemed to snow for days in Syracuse. The winters were cruelly gray and cold. My mother fell on the ice one day during her third year and broke her wrist.

She got a cast, and kept right on wheeling her black book bag to class.

An enrichment for all

She was an inspiration to countless professors, counselors and students. She enriched the school demonstrating that someone her age can handle such a rigorous commitment.

Remember those administrators who had doubts that she could make it full-time? "She proved them all wrong," Ms. Connor said.

My mother did not hesitate to speak up in class. Based on her experiences with my father's company, she can discuss distributorships in her international relations class, and then wheel her black book bag to the next lecture hall to share what she knows about negotiations.

"I admired her viewpoint," said Professor Day.

"She has a good background of life's experiences that I don't have," said Judge Huling.

"She brought the life experiences you couldn't get from a textbook, the stuff of real law," said Professor Micale.

In fact, though Professor Micale has thirty years of international law experience, "She knows more than I do," he said. "When your mother speaks, she becomes the teacher and I become the student."

He said he felt privileged to have had her in his class. "It's just an absolute special treat to me because – and I think the best way I can sum it up is – I can truly become a student in my own class by listening to her, and that is the ultimate."

My mother used to complain that her back bothered her. Luckily, any physical problems my mother had when entering law school began to disappear. In fact, my mother didn't have time to think about her physical ailments. Her back problem miraculously disappeared. So did some of her concerns about the future. "You don't think about getting old or dying while you are busy everyday," my mother said.

Being around young people energized my mother, and her outlook on life brightened. She began to realize that it wasn't healthy for older people to move into retirement homes with other elderly people. It was far better to be around a mix of people who still spoke about joyful things and didn't complain about physical ailments all day.

The benefits ran both ways, too. Not only did my mother feel better about herself, succeeding in younger camp, but those younger students profited from her shared experiences. Her comments about what she had learned from my father's international business experiences piqued their curiosity, Professor Micale said, and "the questions seemed to roll from that point."

Ms. Connor said she "said so many prayers" that my mother would make it through school. But, she added, "her success was based on her determination and conscientiousness. She really worked at it."

The Graduate!

Ms. Connor read my mother's name at the graduation ceremony on May 15th when she graduated at 83. "It enriched my life," said Ms. Connor of the experience. "My hat's off to her."

Professor Micale said he hoped that he had as much vitality as my mother had when he gets to be her age. Another professor said maybe he'd go back to school and study medicine the way he had always wanted.

My mother does not need to work, but she is already checking out the job market with her classmates. She'd like to find a 9-5 job with the government down in Washington, D.C. near four of her children. At her age, she needs a little flex time. "I certainly would not want to work for a big law firm where you work 80 hours per week," she said.

Leave that to the younger grads.

I asked my mom if she had any words of wisdom for other people her age who hadn't yet accomplished what they wanted to in life. She said, "Do whatever you want to do now, not next year or the year after. If you really want to do something, get on the road to achieving your goal today. It is never too late."

Chapter Two:
Why The Older We Get, The Easier It Is To Achieve Our Dreams: The Advantages Of Being Over 50

Most of the men and women whose deeds are described in this book accomplished something phenomenal after the age of 50. That makes sense. Life after 50 is a perfect time to chase after dreams. You simply have more time.

That's because, before the age of 50, you're busy climbing a corporate ladder. Paying the mortgage. Sacrificing for kids to go to college.

Well, after 50, those challenges are often met. You've climbed as high as you want to climb in your profession. The mortgage is paid. (Or, close to it.) Your kids are older or finishing college and are on their way to following their hearts and dreams.

So what about you? Now, more than ever, you have time to do whatever you want to do, time for activities and undertakings you never got around to before. You now can do all the things you want to do because you've done the things you had to do.

Ah, but now you're too old, you tell yourself.

In two words: So what?

Who's to say you can accomplish your goals only

when you're young? If that were true, all the 20- and 30-year-olds would be quite satisfied with their lives.

But they aren't. Not all of them.

Anything is possible. But...

When you're young, you believe that anything is possible and that you can make your dreams come true. Your potential and opportunities seem unlimited.

So how come every young person out there isn't a New York Times best-selling author? A six-figure CEO?

Because youth isn't the key ingredient to achievement. Desire is, and you can have that same desire at the age of 80 that you had at 24.

You'll be older and wiser, too. It has to happen. As you get older, you learn valuable lessons from your life experiences. You know what helps you succeed and what gets in the way of your accomplishment. You can better manage stress so that you can perform on your work-stage. You learn to assess every situation and pick the best course of action.

You're wiser than those starting out in adulthood simply because you've had the benefit of learning from all your mistakes. As far as I'm concerned, the older you get, the more capable you become. And increasingly you may be the most capable person for your dream position. At 80, you could be more competent than a 70-year-old, and at 60 you could be better qualified than someone who's 50.

So don't think of yourself as old. Consider yourself rich! Think of yourself as one of the most capable people around for whatever it is that you want to do. And you might well be! You could be more talented than the 20-year-old out there, but you just haven't proven yourself yet. You could be capable of beating the 30-year-old, but never gave yourself the opportunity.

Aside from the Olympic athlete who may slow down by a few tenths of a second over the years, I think that many of us do a lot of things better as we get older. For one thing, I think that we can concentrate better. Maybe we're less distracted as we get older. That's helpful as well.

We're better, too. George Brunstad - a former pilot whom you'll read about later in this book - believes he may be a little slower at swimming than he was 30 years ago. But he thinks he's got far more endurance now.

I'd also like to think I have improved with age. (I know my wife has. She gets more beautiful every day!) As for me, I believe I'm more athletic. I ran both the Marine Corps Marathon in Washington, D.C. and the Boston Marathon when I was 38. Prior to that, I never ran more than six miles in high school or college.

I also make decisions faster in my 40's. When I was in my 20's and early 30's, I had to spend all my free time reading business books to help steer my company. Today, I don't have to spend as much time reading about the fundamentals of business. I can concentrate on adjusting to the changes instead. I've learned things on my own, running my company with my brother Julian. I could probably write my own book on running a business now.

I don't think I'm the only one capable of doing more later on, either. I think everyone is.

You, too!

Think about yourself. You're rich with experience because you've learned valuable lessons throughout your life. You know that sometimes you win, and sometimes you lose. And, even in those losses, you've had the opportunity to learn what it takes to win.

The spectacular gift: Self-forgiveness

Now you can harvest those life lessons, as Rev. Margaret "Bunny" Voss teaches her students at the Great Lakes Center for Sages in Grand Rapids, Mich. As Rev. Voss says, it's important to take time in your harvest to learn how to forgive. You need to forgive yourself for your shortcomings and your failures. You need to forgive others for any hurt they may have caused you, too. "We work through forgiveness, because forgiveness is a gift we give ourselves," Rev. Voss has explained.

Self-forgiveness certainly is a magnificent gift. Without forgiveness, there can be no achievement. If you can't overlook your foibles, you can't charge ahead. If you can't forgive yourself for falling, you can't pick yourself up and try again. And, if you're filled with bitterness and resentment, you won't have enough positive energy for the good things you want to do.

Every one of us – from the most brilliant NASA scientist to the Pulitzer Prize winning author or journalist, to the most highly-paid CEO – makes mistakes. There isn't one person alive or dead who hasn't made a bad judgment somewhere along the line.

The difference between winners and losers

The difference between winners and losers, though, is that winners forgive themselves. They say, "Okay, I messed up last time, but I think I can succeed next time around." *That's* using the gift of forgiveness!

Failure isn't your enemy. It really is your friend. Failure is your classroom, your mentor, your teacher and guide. With every failure, you learn one of the ingredients for success. You become a bit of an expert at knowing what does and doesn't work.

Even after you've been fired from your last job,

quit the last race, received half a dozen more rejections from publishers and agents, there still is plenty of hope for tomorrow.

As I've learned building my business at Navitar, Inc., "no" is just a minor "no" based on your information as presented today. If you find out what your customer really needs and you keep on showing up and trying, chances are you will ultimately get a "Yes."

Not everything works out right away. My sister, Darice Bailer, is amazed by the number of authors who tell her how many times they were rejected before they got their first book published. Or by famous authors who reveal that even they couldn't sell their last novel to any publishing house.

Everybody fails at one time or another, so get over that. Since you learn many good lessons even when you don't succeed, you still are capable of doing even better work tomorrow. You can leap forward toward your goal.

And no matter how old you are, consider yourself rich!

You're rich with your own gift.

I agree with Rev. Voss that there is a divine spark in each one of us. As she says, each one of us is given a talent to do something that will make life better for others. I believe, as do so many spiritual people of all faiths, that God designed it that way. I believe God built us that way because he has special plans for each of us. I also believe God may want us to struggle a bit along the way so that, when we finally accomplish whatever it is that he – and we – want to do, we'll appreciate it.

Only when we overcome our fears or anxieties in the darkness of despair can we truly bask in the glory of that ultimate achievement.

And, it is coming!

In fact, it might be just around the corner. Read on!

Chapter Three
This Book Was Written For You!

This book is written for anyone in any stage of life. It's for anyone who hears the inner rumblings of a dream. You could be retired and bored. You could be in the middle of a mid-life crisis. You could be 20 or 30.

Doing what you want to do may be difficult at first, but it will also be hugely rewarding.

The fact that you are ready ... no, make that *willing* ... to change direction means you're getting closer to where you want to go. And, no matter how old you are, you can get there.

Which category fits you?

A) Retired and bored – Want to get back into the work world? You can do it.

It's a myth that when you get older your mind deteriorates. My mother, in her 80's, was getting A's and B's in law school courses that younger students could barely pass. Her eyes may be less sharp than they used to, but not her mind.

If you feel a twitch in your heart to accomplish

something, then there is nothing to prevent you from doing so. My mother proves this every day. Many older people are living rewarding lives even at 70, 80, 90, or 100. It is up to you to make that happen for yourself.

Aim high, too! I know my parents always did (you've read about my Mom ... my Dad also has a chapter in this book), and they expected their kids to do the same. Believe you can accomplish what you want, for your life is a self-fulfilling prophecy.

Many of my relatives are in their 70's and 80's, and they expect to follow their passions until it's time to go. Doing something fulfilling certainly is helping my aunts and uncles live longer. It's as simple and as profound as this: if you are doing something that makes you happy, then your mental well-being will contribute to your physical well-being. Medical researchers are now saying that laughter helps keep the mind and body fit. It eases tension, reduces stress, and actually releases infection-fighting antibodies.

Have you ever wondered why the great comedians like Bob Hope, George Burns, and Milton Berle lived so long? Maybe it's because they laughed hard and long each day! They did what they enjoyed – performing in front of audiences and making others happy.

Journalist Norman Cousins commented in his book *Anatomy of an Illness* that if a person is cheerful all the time, and if there is love, faith and hope inside him, then that individual should overcome sickness. If stress, anxiety, fear, and worry pull a man down, then faith, hope, love, and laughter will surely lift him up. Laughter has been shown to ease depression and a whole host of ailments.

My mother-in-law, Nieves Olemberg, is 69 and has arthritis in most of her joints. She has been told by her doctor that she needs a double knee replacement. But she doesn't complain. She likes to do volunteer work in the community, and she says she is too busy to feel any pain! There is medical proof of what she says, too. Endorphins are chemicals produced in the brain, acting like morphine and other pain relievers. The word endorphin, in fact, is an abbreviation of "endogenous morphine," or morphine produced naturally in the body. (Not to worry: if it's habit-forming, it's one of the best habits you can ever absorb.)

If you're lucky enough to find work fulfilling and enriching for you, you help your body produce endorphins. Those endorphins will build up your immune system, keep brain cells young and healthy, and improve your memory. That may be why Grandma Jeanette is doing so well at law school!

Maybe this book will help you relax and do something you've always wanted. Joy isn't always found at the same fountain. Some people feel good making their family happy by cooking delicious meals and keeping the house clean. Others want to get out and coach a youth basketball team or volunteer at a local museum. Still others want to dabble in a second career and strike a balance between work, family and free time.

Then again, some people have never been lucky enough to find that balance. They've been working long hours making ends meet and never have had time to spend an afternoon fishing or getting a facial with the ladies at a local spa. Those who feel they've been missing out on these pleasures in life may choose to take it easy in retirement ... even sitting in the hammock and reading a good book!

Make sure you don't die of boredom. Make sure that when it is time to go, you leave with a smile on your face. If that smile comes from quality time with family and friends, that is more than ok. You may also want to try a second career in something totally different while ensuring that this time around, work hours will be mixed with quality family time and free time. The Rule of Double Success will work for you:

If you're successful once in a particular field, the chance of success a second time around increases exponentially.

B) Middle to Late in a Career, Midlife crisis? Want a different career? Haven't done anything meaningful yet? You can do it.

The positive news on midlife is that the baby boom generation has postponed it. I believe firmly that whereas formerly the midlife crisis struck at 40, now it hits around 50. That's because years ago, people got married at 20 and had their children fairly young. The nest was empty in one's early 40's.

Today, millions of men and women are just getting around to buying an engagement ring at 35. The house won't empty for many years after that! Today, it's common for 50-year-olds to wonder what they want to do with the rest of their lives and take stock of whether they've accomplished all that they wanted.

A midlife crisis is a time when someone assesses what they've done so far with their life and where they'd like to be. They start to face up to things they've repressed in order to please other people. Maybe they'd like to ditch the first career and switch to something more fulfilling. But how? These men and women may be the family's chief income producer, the one who earns what it takes to send the kids to private school now and on to college later.

A friend of mine is an obstetrician who feels trapped in obstetrics although he'd much rather give it up. He's lost his love for patients, because he never knows which one will turn on him and sue. The trust and rapport he once felt is gone. Plus, he's tired of staying up every third night. His 40-year-old body just can't take it anymore without sleep.

But how can he leave obstetrics, he wonders? He feels trapped into staying to pay off the malpractice insurance, the mortgage, and all his kids' tuitions. He isn't happy, but he wonders how his family will be able to afford all the comforts of the past if he changes jobs.

Luckily, this obstetrician's wife is very supportive. She tells him they can move to a smaller house and get by ... just so long as he's happy. Here we have a couple who really are a *couple*, not just two people living together. This physician's wife is happy to swap a house, car, vacation - you name it - for her husband's happiness. If you feel trapped in your profession, why not talk to your spouse about your feelings?

If you feel stuck in a career that long ago lost its joy for you, think about all the years ahead. Your life is far from over and you *can* make a change. There still is time to do what really interests you. For whatever reason you haven't followed your dream career by now, but it would be a shame to wait another day. Since we're all living longer, midlife should be viewed as an opportunity to make changes for the better. It can be a springboard to Utopia.

Let go of your fears for the future and give yourself a chance to try something new.

C) 20-30+ years old? Just getting started? Don't let youth be wasted on the young. You have the opportunity to prevent future boredom.

Even if you're in your 20's or 30's and are just getting started, don't put off your dream. Make a change if you need to, and do it soon. When you're young, the future seems like forever. You almost feel as if you will live forever, and that there is plenty of time and miles of road ahead. But as you get older and watch a parent, relative, sibling or friend die, you realize that the future isn't guaranteed. Each day is precious because no one knows when it will be his or her last. And once that realization sets in, you want to spend your time with the people who make you happy and the pursuits that enrich your life.

D) What does this all mean?
It's as simple as this: live your life. Enjoy your life. Don't let yourself be trapped in a life of quiet desperation. It's *your* life. Stay in charge.

Chapter Four
Believe In Yourself ... With A Little Help From Family And Friends.

(A short but important chapter.)

Some people just naturally believe in themselves and will try something new, truly believing that they will ultimately succeed in their task. These individuals don't need any more conversation on this subject. They genuinely believe in themselves and are not deterred by naysayers.

If you're one of the "others," you'll need to learn about believing in yourself; and you probably will need a lot of support from family and friends.

You also will need to avoid hanging out with negative people. There will be many people who will say you're too old ... not smart enough ... not capable enough ...not this or that. "You haven't done it in the past, why do you think that you can do it now?"

Comments like these can affect your attitude, so just let them go in one ear and out the other. Stress the good things and accomplishments you have achieved. Emphasize the positive and avoid the negative. Just because you haven't done whatever in the past, that certainly doesn't mean that you can't do it in the future. Regardless of who you are, I'm telling you that anyone can accomplish what he or she wants, given the desire, the time, and a relentless spirit to overcome any obstacles that may be thrown in your way.

Believing in yourself is the key for anyone to achieve their dreams. For some, it just comes naturally. For others, it can still be a learned skill. People like Anthony Robbins are masters of helping people believe in themselves. I personally listened to and enjoyed his twelve tape series entitled "Personal Power." It helped me. The "Personal Power" course will open the possibilities in life and unlock the power and potential already inside of you! And that's just one of many sources of help. There are many other motivational books and tapes on the market. It doesn't matter which you choose as long as you gain the strength to go after your dreams.

Are you the second type of person, one who needs to learn belief and needs a little support from family in friends? Don't worry, you can also be equally successful. You just first have to recognize what you desire and then get all the tools necessary for success. It might be attending one of the many "Success Seminars." Once you belief in yourself, you then can attain the knowledge to do the task you dream of. Research the subject matter or plunge into whatever training is required. When you find information starts to repeat itself, then it's time to go into action. After all, knowledge without action is useless.

With or without help, don't quit. Don't.

You may be like many people, without the benefit of secure finances in the bank. You may have to depend on your spouse to bring in the steady income while your dreams and ideas take time to develop. If you have a supportive spouse, you can do it. If your spouse is less supportive, it will be a lot more difficult or take more time, but don't give up. You still can do anything, provided you don't stop working on it. Believe that you will live to over 100. Break down your goals into small easily achievable steps. You'll find yourself getting to where you want to be.

It will be up to you to say, "I am going to do it" and think about how rewarding it will be when you can look back at the days when you were struggling or a little less fulfilled. You soon will be content and happy knowing that you truly did achieve your dreams and are living an enriched and fulfilled life.

Chapter Five
The Retirement Years:
A Chance To Begin Anew

Baby boomers have always asked questions. As teenagers and young adults they wondered: why could men have careers and not women? Why was war better than peace? Boomers wanted to change the world when they were younger. Not much has changed now that they're older, either!

And what a lot of baby boomers there are. Some 76 million were born between 1946 and 1964, when the "boom" unofficially ended.

The baby boomers aren't aging without a fight. For the pre-World War II generation, retirement meant retiring from one's life-long profession. Some, like ex-coal miners, could no longer physically continue working down in the mines. Others from that generation simply felt the time was right to quit. It was time to hold a grandchild's hand or play a round of bridge.

Yet millions upon millions of baby boomers have already turned 50, and they would like to retire that whole notion of withdrawing from work.

Baby boomers, you see, have greater life expectancies and expectations than their grandparents. They easily might live 25 years after they retire, whereas their grandparents might have expected to live five or ten. Twenty-five years is a long time to sit there watching the sun set.

So, with that longevity possible, many boomers see retirement as a beginning, not an end. Eighty percent of this post-war generation expects to keep working past the age of 65. And government statistics show that the percentage of people over 65 still in the work force has been rising over the past ten years. Many people work because they want to.

Of course, not all boomers have the luxury of choosing whether or not to show up at the office. Many corporations have cut pensions, health insurance, and retirement benefits. So some older employees can't afford to retire.

But many baby boomers continue working because they want to stay connected and feel useful. They don't hesitate to learn new skills and change fields, either.

Retirement = New Start.

According to an AARP report on Americans over 50, two-thirds of all 50- to 75-year-olds view retirement as a chance to begin anew with new goals and activities. This graying population sees retirement as a chance to reinvent, not quit. They see retirement as a chance to go back to school, learn a new profession, and take on a whole new field. This generation wants to rock on.

And why shouldn't they? The current AARP membership is healthier than any group of the past, and the generation after them – Generation X – is 10 percent smaller. That means Generation X can't fill all the jobs the boomers leave. As boomers retire, who will replace them ... not to mention filling all the new jobs, either?

"Our research tells us that older workers will continue to have a prominent and increasing role in the labor force in the coming decades. And, they will step up and fill the jobs that are most likely to need workers," said John Rother, AARP director of policy and strategy, in the Northern Colorado Business Report.

(An indication of the changing playing field: AARP no longer refers to itself as The American Association of *Retired* Persons.)

The boomers are fit and ready. But, whereas their parents just worked to make a living, the boomers need more meaning in their lives. In fact, according to an AARP survey, half of all adults of retirement age plan to volunteer in retirement. They want to make a difference in someone's life.

"The times, they are a-changin'!"

As Bob Dylan sang back in the 1960's, "The times, they are a-changin'!" In 1950, fewer than half of all men over 65 kept on working. But, half of the 35 million AARP members work today, either part or full-time.

My mother, who is 83, is one of those 35 million AARP members who will continue to work. She is just one example of many elderly people going back to school to start anew. I think my mother is evidence of the trend in which many older people fill seats in university lecture halls. Some just like to keep on learning. Others want to study new skills.

After all, with a longer life expectancy, life after 50 or 60 is our chance for a second whirl. Parents have worked to send their children to college. Now, they can send themselves. They may have paid off the mortgage by now along with the children's tuition, so they might have more money to enroll in a course that interests them. Perhaps they want to learn how to write a book, open a restaurant, or practice law. With children grown, this post-50 generation can now focus on itself.

And if the over-50 crowd wants to keep on working, companies are accommodating them. AARP isn't the only source of reports about more and more companies with friendly policies for their older crew.

Douglas Martin wrote in *The New York Times* that companies like Wal-Mart, McDonald's and the CVS drugstore chain are making an aggressive effort to hire the elderly. Firms recognize that older workers are more reliable and experienced and have just as much ability to learn new skills. Companies are taking advantage of the availability of older employees and potential employees who want to work, by offering not only further development training but often tuition reimbursement at local universities. Companies are also becoming more flexible, giving older employees a chance to work part-time or telecommute.

All in the family

My brother and I run a diversified optical technology company called Navitar. My father worked into his 80's, but that wasn't the only reason we feel older workers are extremely valuable. At Navitar, we've always had the policy that anyone who wanted to work for us could, no matter whether the employee was 60, 70, or 80.

My brother Julian and I believe older workers should be able to work as long as they want and in any capacity. I fondly remember one employee named Eugene Turula. Gene was our leading optical engineer and a brilliant designer. Gene had been with our company for more than 25 years and wanted to keep on working. But he also wanted to slow down a bit and spend more time with his family. Though Gene was born in a previous era, Gene acted as a typical baby boomer. He wanted to continue in his career ... but understandably, not on a 9-5 treadmill.

So we set up a schedule enabling Gene to work fewer days. And Gene, like my father, worked until the end. He came in to the office one day a week until he died at age 83. I believe he lived a longer and more fulfilled life because of his work. He was a precious asset to our company and we all miss him dearly.

The point: Gene didn't have to work. He *wanted* to work. And Navitar and most forward-thinking employers need dedicated employees like him, especially as lower birth rates reduce the number of workers available to fill new jobs. For the first time in American history, we are nearing the time when there are more old folks than young folks.

Yet those "old" folk sure know how to stay young. This book is for them. And you. Sooner or later, it's for all of us.

To Mary

Dreams do come true
Be sure you live yours.
Love, Margaret

Chapter Six
Margaret Hagerty, Champion Runner

Margaret Hagerty didn't start running until she neared the finish line. That's when, at the age of 64, Margaret was told by her doctor to quit smoking or face an early death. Not wanting to leave this world too soon, Margaret enrolled in a stop smoking clinic. She vowed to give up her old habit. What happened next is incredible.

The day after she started attending the clinic, Margaret had a nicotine fit. She bounced around, full of nervous energy. To keep herself from lighting up one more cigarette, Margaret flew out of the house and bolted down the street. A runner was born. Margaret decided she liked running. She joined a local running club. At first, her objective was just to keep up. After all, the other runners were half her age and twice her speed. The average age of the runner group members was 35 to 40. The other runners were very supportive of Margaret, though. They told her they wanted to be just like her when they "grew up."

When Margaret heard a friend talk about something called the New York Marathon, she began to wonder. Could she run a marathon, too? The New York Marathon is more than 26 miles of solid running. The television news regularly shows contestants dropping, from exhaustion.

Margaret asked some of her friends what they thought. Had she seen her psychiatrist lately, her friends asked? They were only kidding, though, and were very supportive of Margaret's preparations for her first 26.2-mile run. To build up the endurance she would need for the feat, Margaret ran up and down the main street in her home town of Concord, North Carolina. It took her just about all day to cover 26.2 miles, but she did it. She was elated, too. She phoned a friend: "I told her that I can now do the New York Marathon," Margaret said.

Margaret completed her first marathon a little bit farther south, in Greensboro, North Carolina. "It was a piece of cake," Margaret said. "I loved every minute of it." As she neared the finish line, the director of the race told Margaret to slow down. She had already set a state record in her age group. "I didn't want to slow down. I felt great," Margaret said.

Margaret headed north and entered the New York City Marathon. Result? She's completed at least seventy marathons since.

Now, what to do with those old knees? Become a triathlete.

Running all those marathons took its toll on

Margaret's legs. At 69, Margaret's left knee started to hurt and she had to back off running for a while. The pain became so sharp she needed crutches to walk.

After crying one afternoon because she thought her running career was over, Margaret grabbed her towel and bathing suit and swam laps at the local YMCA. If she couldn't run, she could at least swim. That way she could maintain the cardiovascular strength she'd built up over the past few years.

Margaret entered some United States Master's Swim races and set an age group record in the mile in her state. With time and all that water therapy, Margaret's knee healed. She now had a swimming weapon to add to her running, which made her an ideal triathlete candidate. After all, she could now complete the swimming portion of the swim-bike-run race. Margaret's first objective was just to get out there and do the three-stage event.

She was understandably tired in the middle of her first one. "When I got off the bike, my legs did not want to run," Margaret said. Still, "I did the best I could," she said. She completed her first triathlon and decided to sign up for another one, aiming to do a little better the next time around. Margaret won a gold medal at a Senior Olympics triathlon in Baton Rouge, Louisiana. She became a national age group champion during her competition, as well.

Taking up swimming had been a very good move.

"Turn an obstacle into a plus and don't let it be a minus," Margaret advises others. "Sometimes you can sidestep an obstacle and achieve an objective by not giving up."

Sixteen years and many triathlons later, Margaret is still running. She works for Marathon Tours and has run marathons in Greece, Australia, and Africa. She always wanted to travel, having been envious when a former retired coworker mailed her postcards from abroad. Margaret wants to see the Great Wall of China. Why not? Perhaps she'll run a marathon there.

Being 60 or 70 never bothered Margaret, but she is beginning to think that 80 is a little old. Not that she's slowing down any, mind you. Margaret is quick to say that you just can't think about your age. "It's just a number," she said. "You have to keep on going."

"You don't know what is possible ... until you try the impossible."

Although it now is harder for Margaret to run marathons than it was sixteen years ago when she first started, she wants to stay at it. Her body resists at times and craves for her to slow down and walk, but Margaret is going to run for as long as she can. When the time comes that she just can't run another step, she'll deal with it. She's prepared.

Margaret has plenty of advice for those who are thinking about running marathons or trying to achieve other goals in life. "You don't know what is possible until you try the impossible," she said.

She even likes to quote the late actress Helen Hayes. "Self doubt and fear of failure are the leg irons that keep us chained to the wailing wall of un-accomplishment."

Margaret believes everyone should at least forge ahead and try new things. "Even if you fail, you are not going to have to live with it as long as you'd have to live with the automatic failure of not trying," she says.

And *you* will find yourself pleased and proud of the person you have become from your new-found talents and achievements. As Oliver Wendell Holmes once said, "Man's mind, once stretched by a new idea, never regains its original dimension."

Chapter Seven
Dr. Gail Fredericks, Unlikely M.D.

Gail Fredericks was a little late at making house calls. After all, she didn't become a family doctor until she was 51! In fact, when Gail earned her medical degree in 1993, she was the oldest medical school graduate in University of Maryland history.

So, what took her so long to use a stethoscope?

Well, Gail Fredericks married when she was a 20-year-old student at Immaculate Heart College Center in Los Angeles. A year later, in 1963, she dropped out of school after her daughter Wendy was born. Two years later, when Wendy was a toddler, Gail and her husband separated. Soon, they divorced and Gail was a young single mother.

Gail didn't think about becoming a doctor back then. All she could think of was, "How do I support my daughter?" Luckily, Gail's parents had taught her that it was important to work hard and take great satisfaction in working toward something and achieving it.

Over the next ten years, Gail took care of Wendy during the day and worked as a cocktail waitress at night. She also managed to complete her college degree and earn a master's degree, too. Eventually, Gail took a job with the Social Security Administration in Reno, Nevada. She worked there for years during the day, continuing to moonlight as a cocktail waitress. After all, she needed to pay off the mortgage and the orthodontist.

In 1974, Gail's mother was diagnosed with lung cancer. Over the next two years her mother would suffer through chemotherapy and radiation before dying. It was then, in 1976, at the age of 34, that Gail decided that she wanted to become a doctor.

Why? Gail felt she could have done a better job caring for her mother than the doctors had. "I don't know if they did a bad job," she said, and admitted that "it is very hard to give people bad news." But, while her mother's doctors would level with Gail and tell her that her mother was terminal and that there was no hope of a cure, they left it to Gail to break the news to her mother. The burden was on her.

"I don't think that's fair to the family," Gail said. "At least I would have the courage to say to somebody, 'Here is your diagnosis.' I think it's very important to give people that information, to say that this is a very serious disease and you don't have any curative treatment for it." Gail wanted to be a physician and tend not only to physical wounds but the subsequent emotional ones as well. She wanted to learn from her mother's experience and become a better caregiver.

A 47-year-old freshman

So, in 1976, after her mother's death, Gail approached the University of Nevada School of Medicine in Reno. She asked about applying, although she understood she was 34 and a dozen years older than the traditional college senior making inquiries.

The University of Nevada, like most medical schools in the country, had never accepted a woman in her 30's. There were four years of medical school to complete and several years of internship and residency, depending on the chosen specialty. How many years could a prospective physician in her 30's really expect to practice? The medical school that would grant a diploma to this older student "couldn't count on getting a payback in the sense of service," Gail said. "They figured that somebody this old would not be able to give them the return someone in their 20's would give."

But, those medical schools didn't know Gail. "I intended to practice for a long, long time," she said.

Still, Gail didn't quite meet all the course requirements for medical school. Gail had been an English major in college, and she lacked such courses as biochemistry and organic chemistry. She also didn't have the transcript of a scholastic star. But beyond all that, she was, well, old!

The University of Nevada was hardly encouraging. Gail moped around for ten years, still wanting to go to medical school but feeling like the dream was less likely with every passing birthday. Finally, a friend got tired of listening to Gail wistfully say that she wished she could go to medical school and asked, "Gail, did you ever try?" Well, come to think of it, Gail's friend was right. She never did actually apply.

"I might as well try," Gail thought. So, after letting her friend's words percolate in her mind for another year, Gail went back to all the medical admissions people who said that she would never get in and asked them what courses she needed to take.

The admissions staff said she could take all the courses she wanted but that she wouldn't get in. And, even if by some miracle she did get in, the school didn't think she'd end up practicing medicine. She'd end up as a hospital administrator instead.

"That's okay, but I need to try," Gail said.

Gail's daughter was her biggest cheerleader, and always believed that her mom could do it. "Go for it," Gail's daughter and close friends said. "You only get one chance to live, so you just might as well try."

Since the University of Nevada School of Medicine admissions staff would not tell Gail what courses she lacked, Gail went to the library. She looked up the statistics from the previous year's entering class, and determined what courses she still needed on her transcript. Then, she signed up to take them, and, one by one, began knocking them off. After the first two years of study, she ran into a roadblock. There were no more courses offered at night. The ones she still needed were only taught during the day.

Well, let her go take them, Gail's bosses said. Especially after they saw how serious she was about becoming a doctor. So, for the next year and a half, Gail worked part-time and completed her course requirements.

Then, she signed up for Stanley Kaplan classes to prepare her for the Medical-College Admissions test or MCAT. Gail knew that doing well on the MCAT was going to be very important or schools would not look at her.

And so, in 1989, when she was in her late 40's, Gail trekked off to her MCAT preparatory classes after work. She listened to the tapes and took the practice tests while the Stanley Kaplan staff prepared to go home. She ended up locking up the office, because she was the last one there. "I would stay and I would work to 10:00 or 11:00 p.m. every night all summer long because I was going to pass that sucker," Gail said. "I knew that I had to do well on the MCAT's or the schools would not look at me no matter how good my grades were."

Gail applied to 14 medical schools. Very few people expected her to get in, and people said they hated to see her waste all that time and money. Gail thought that if no American medical school accepted her, she could always apply to a foreign school. "One way or another, I was going to get in," she said.

Lo and behold, the University of Maryland at Baltimore accepted Gail Fredericks. In the end, it was Gail Frederick's perseverance that swayed the admissions staff in her favor. The university recognized that the same commitment Gail demonstrated in getting in was going to help her succeed in school. "They were so wonderful," Gail said.

So in 1990, at the age of 47, Gail Fredericks started medical school at the University of Maryland at Baltimore. Finally, she was heading toward her dream. Her daughter Wendy teased her. "In most families, the kids grow up and go away to school, but in my family, the kid grew up and the mom went away to school!"

Not only that, but mom went to medical school with students younger than her daughter! Gail didn't mind being twice as old as the other students, though. "One of the nice things is that the other kids miss their folks," she said. "I was able to be a maternal kind of person in a lot of situations. And, it worked out well." Students even elected Gail class treasurer for four years!

Getting accepted to medical school was a big hurdle, but staying in was, too. Gail had no free time and no disposable income. She found herself with about 2½ hours a week to take care of grocery shopping, showers, and so forth. She also didn't have much money after paying for tuition, books and living expenses at school. "In medical school it all goes one way," she said. "It's expensive, and you never know if you're going to make it." Eating hot dogs became a luxury for Gail. "When hot dogs are a treat, you're in trouble," she joked.

With age comes understanding

As difficult as it was, Gail believes that there were advantages to going back to school later in life. "The main advantage is that you have a lot more life experiences to draw on," she says. Since Gail had been a patient longer than she had been a doctor, she understands that patients don't like to wait in doctors' offices. She tries not to keep anyone waiting, and apologizes when she's late. She understands the indignity of those hospital gowns, too.

And since she lost her mother to cancer, Gail understands what some of her own patients are going through.

Gail doesn't regret her years of struggle. "All the bad things, all the things that you failed at, all the discouraging things... all those things bring you to the place where you say 'I am going to do this.' And if you don't have all the failures and all the discouraging things that happen earlier, I don't think that you get to that point. It doesn't make any of those bad things easier, but if you don't have those experiences, I don't think you get to the point where you can make the commitment to what you are going to do and go for it."

Gail is glad she did. She loves being a doctor and feels very blessed. "I cannot tell you how much I love what I do," she said. "It is such a gift to be able to get up in the morning and do what I want to do. I'm in family practice, and I have one family where I'm taking care of three generations. Today I visited a 99-year-old lady who couldn't get in to see me."

"I am so fortunate that I love my life and I have not always felt that way. It's beautiful to be able to say that if the good fairy said, 'Okay, you can redo your life now,' I wouldn't want to change anything. I would take the hard times, the bad times, the sad times, and the good times ... because they helped me get through to where I am today."

Asked if she had any words of wisdom for others trying to achieve their dream, Gail replied, "Each of us needs to find something that makes us feel of use, of service, and that in some way we can make a positive contribution to the universe. I don't care what that may be. It doesn't have to be law or medicine. It could be anything, and sometimes it takes a while to find what you want. Just don't give up. There are a lot of things out there that the world can benefit from."

She certainly proved that!

Chapter Eight
George Brunstad, English Channel Swimmer

On his 69th birthday, George Brunstad told his family not to throw him any more birthday parties. He was getting too old.

Not that he looked it, mind you. George was a retired American Airlines pilot and could have passed for a young Charles Lindbergh. He was tall and lean with sandy brown hair, like Lucky Lindy himself.

Well, if he didn't want any more parties, what did George want to do when he turned 70, his family asked?

Off the cuff, George said, "Swim the English Channel."

George was serious, too. He'd been a varsity swimmer at Washington State University in his youth, and he'd won over one hundred U.S. Masters National Championship races as an adult.

But, swimming across the 21-mile channel is like climbing Mount Everest. It's the pinnacle of mental and physical accomplishment when it comes to swimming. Heck, it feels about as cold as climbing Mount Everest, too. The water temperature out there in the Straits of Dover is about 58 to 62 degrees Fahrenheit.

It's hardly the Caribbean, and at that temperature it feels like one is swimming in a tub of melting ice. You burn about 800 calories an hour and could die of hypothermia.

You can't wear a wet suit to protect yourself, either.

George had crossed the Channel plenty of times flying Boeing 767's for American Airlines during his career. But he'd never dipped a toe in the Channel, much less tried to swim it. George would be the oldest person in the world to try, much less succeed.

"Unless I face the challenge and take the risk, I'll never know what I can do," George wrote in his journal.

At one of his master's swim championships, George approached Thomas Hetzel, a man who swum the Channel at least eight times. George asked Thomas if he thought he could do it.

Thomas said yes.

A couple of months passed, and then George had a vision in bed one night. He was one of those people who believe that windows of opportunity come along only once in a lifetime, and that you can never achieve anything great unless you take risks and try.

George had flown across the Atlantic many times for American Airlines. But, Lindbergh was the one in the history books because he had been the first.

Well, maybe George could be the first 70-year-old

to swim that Channel. Maybe he could even raise money for charity, too.

Danger, for a noble cause

George wanted to raise money to build an orphanage, medical center, school, mission and church in Haiti. He'd been there with his Wilton, Connecticut Baptist Church, and he wanted to do something for the poor people in that country. Maybe people would sponsor him during his training and donate money to that cause. George was a deacon of his church and a very spiritual person. He was dedicated to the glory of God and admired people who were strong and religious, too.

People like his parents, Abraham Lincoln, Martin Luther King, Nelson Mandela, Billy Graham and Mother Theresa. People who were leaders during difficult times.

Well, swimming across that Channel would certainly be difficult. And George knew he'd need human as well as spiritual guidance. He started asking former Channel swimmers what it was like, and he found that crossing the Channel was indeed as risky as climbing Mount Everest.

As an example – the water temperature. George taught swimming lessons in a Wilton YMCA pool that was like a warm bathtub - about 86 degrees. The Channel was almost 30 degrees colder.

Then there was the factor of tides. The Channel was only swimmable from late July to early September, and even then weather conditions often made crossing on those days impossible.

The tide changed direction every six hours. Though the distance was 21 miles from Dover, England to Cap Gris Nez, France, the current could roll you off course so you ended up weaving back and forth several miles longer than that. All in all, it might take George 14 to 15 hours to get across.

He'd be batted around pretty badly and stung by jellyfish, too. The weather was harsh in that part of the ocean, and waves swelled up into violent white caps. The waves could whip up to eight or ten feet tall, making you feel like you were out in the middle of the Bermuda Triangle. Swimmers who reached the other side shivered uncontrollably for hours. A man George's age could succumb to a heart attack or stroke.

George didn't think about any of that. In a journal that friends had given him to record his thoughts as he embarked on his challenge of a lifetime, George wrote down a quote from Henry David Thoreau: "Go confidently in the direction of your dreams."

The right stuff

To get in shape to swim across the Channel, George started training 12 hours a week. He was accustomed to getting up at 4:30 each morning to open the Wilton YMCA pool an hour later. Then he'd work as a lifeguard and swim instructor throughout the day finding time to slip into the Y's 50-meter pool and swim laps himself.

Back and forth he would go in the Y pool. He'd log over three miles on Monday's and do speed work on Wednesday's. On Friday's, he planned to build up to swimming 20,000 meters, or over twelve miles! Phew. If that weren't enough, he'd work out in the fitness center on Tuesday's and Thursday's, too!

George skipped the warm showers after his training and kept the faucet on cold instead. He wanted to get used to the 58-degree water he'd be swimming in the following summer. In May and June of 2004, he'd start swimming in Long Island Sound. Then, during the summer, he planned to swim several hours a day in the Atlantic Ocean off the coast of Maine while vacationing with his family. Some of these swims might be six or eight hours long. All that cold ocean water would acclimatize George to what he would face when he walked out into the Channel to start his swim right around his 70th birthday – on August 25, 2004.

George felt he had the right stuff to cross the Channel at his age. He was a U.S. Master's Swimming All-Star, winning an award given to only one swimmer in each age group each year. The All-Star ranking meant he had accumulated the most points and won the most swim races.

He'd won every national long distance championship in his age group. There are five national open water championships a year, and George had won them all. He'd won both world championships (the 3K and 5K events), too. In 2003, he won four national championship open water swims and was second in four. He lost only to ex-Olympians.

The oldest man ever to swim across the English Channel wasn't an Olympian but an Australian swimmer named Clifford Batts. Batts was 67 on August 19, 1987 when he completed his crossing in 18 hours and 37 minutes.

Now it might be George's turn to stroke his way into the Guinness Book of World Records. After all, George likes to quote Walt Disney: "If you can dream it, you can do it."

There was one final quote that George liked, and it came from evangelist Bruce Wilkinson: "Your Father knows you immediately, and He has already given you strategic opportunities, passions, interests and capabilities. These are the starting points for how He will touch the world through you."

George hoped to do just that with his Channel swim.

Chapter Nine
Grandma Moses, Late-Blooming Artist

Anna Mary Robertson "Grandma" Moses didn't think she was special, even thought the rest of the world did. "Anybody can paint," Mrs. Moses explained to journalist Edward R. Murrow when he interviewed her on television.

If anybody could paint the sweet, homey farm pictures that Mrs. Moses did, then anyone could start late in life, too. For Grandma Moses didn't take up painting as a hobby until she was a 76-year-old grandmother. Then, she didn't stop. She exhibited at her first show when she was 79, and she completed over one thousand oil canvases before she died in 1961 at the age of 101. Twenty-five of those thousand paintings were created *after* she turned 100.

Grandma Moses started out creating farm scenes with worsted wool. She had to stop embroidering, though, because her fingers were too gnarled and crippled for her to slip the embroidery needle through a canvas any longer. Her hands ached from rheumatoid arthritis, and the pain kept her awake at night.

As was typical throughout her life, Mrs. Moses didn't complain. She accepted her condition and shrugged. If she couldn't embroider her beloved farm scenes any longer, then maybe there was another hobby she could take up that would bring her that same joy.

Historic advice

"I think you could paint better and faster than you could do worsted pictures," Mrs. Moses recalled her sister saying.

So Mrs. Moses dabbed a paintbrush in a can of ordinary oil paint and tried. No one taught Grandma Moses how to mix the paints or create her farm life scenes. She taught herself, and through her art she brought her warmth and goodness to the rest of the nation.

Mrs. Moses appeared on the covers of Time and Life magazine, becoming the best-known female painter of her time. Her portraits of rural America were reproduced on dinnerware and Hallmark Christmas cards. Hallmark sold millions of cards, and the art work of the tiny gray-haired artist was embraced by American presidents and people around the world.

Painting the world she knew and loved

Grandma Moses created simple, cozy pictures about life on the farm. She had grown up on a farm and worked on a farm and knew that life well. There were sleigh rides and quilting bees. There were berries to pick, apple butter to churn, and turkeys to catch for a Thanksgiving feast. Mrs. Moses painted from memory. And, from the look of her paintings, her memories were happy ones. After all, the little men, women and children in a Grandma Moses paintings are always smiling. One can picture *her* smiling as she brought brush to canvas.

"I was happy and contented," Grandma Moses wrote in her 1951 autobiography, *My Life's History*. "I knew nothing better and made the best out of what life offered. And life is what we make it, always has been, always will be."

If painting hadn't replaced embroidery as her hobby, Mrs. Moses said she would have tried something else. "If I didn't start painting, I would have raised chickens," Grandma Moses told Mr. Murrow. "I would never sit back in a rocking chair, waiting for someone to help."

An American life – tragedies and triumphs

That self-reliant attitude was bred in a large family. Anna Mary Robertson was born September 7, 1860 in upstate New York. She was one of ten children, and her father encouraged her to paint as a child. But, that passion, along with her schooling and her childhood were cut short when she left home to work fulltime as a farm hand at the age of 12. At the age of 27, Anna married a fellow farm hand named Thomas Salmon Moses. She gave birth to ten children, but only five lived to walk. She glossed over hardship and tragedy throughout her life.

Some of her children lived and some died.

Her husband died, too. Grandma Moses started painting shortly before her beloved husband passed away. In her autobiography, she recalled him saying that her paintings were "real good." After Mr. Moses left the world a few weeks later, painting helped overcome Mrs. Moses' grief, because she felt like he was right there with her, watching over her.

Grandma Moses tried to sell her paintings at local drugstores and pharmacies. A New York City civil engineer and art collector named Louis Caldor happened to see a couple of her paintings in a drug store window in Hoosick Falls, N.Y. and bought all of them. They cost just $3 to $5, depending on how big they were.

Mr. Caldor told Grandma Moses he'd make her famous. He did, too. The following year, Grandma Moses' artwork appeared in a show of contemporary self-taught painters at the Museum of Modern Art in New York. In 1940, Grandma Moses' paintings were displayed at New York's Gimbel's Department Store and the Gallerie St. Etienne.

Grandma Moses never tried to model her art work after the master painters such as Michelangelo or Leonardo Da Vinci. She remained true to herself, painting her world as she had known it. She painted while sitting next to her washer and dryer, and her paintings reflected her spirit of optimism, love and joy. "What's the use of painting a picture if it isn't something nice?" she once said.

In Grandma Moses' world, life was simple and life was good. The World War exploding overseas and the Cold War that followed didn't darken her spirit.

At the time of her death, Grandma Moses' paintings hung in nine museums in the United States and in Paris and Vienna. She brought joy to millions of people, just as she had brought quiet satisfaction to herself.

Chapter Ten
Ray Kroc, The Hamburger King

Whether he was 20 or 50, Ray Kroc never hesitated to seize the day. As the founder of the giant McDonald's fast food chain said in his autobiography, *Grinding it Out*, a man must take advantage of any opportunity that comes along.

Ray did, even when he was older.

Ray opened his first McDonald's franchise in 1954, when he was 52. Compared to other American billionaires and how old they were when they started their corporations, that's late.

Some successful individuals might even have retired in their 50's.

Not Ray Kroc. Ray was still full of ambition, and he chased after every opportunity. He was an optimist. He never looked back, thinking his best years were behind him. Instead, Ray always believed that the best was yet to come.

Ray's mother called him Danny Dreamer. He was always day dreaming about some scheme to make money, even as a young boy. When Ray was 4, a phrenologist (a person who believed he could judge a man's character by the shape of his skull) predicted that Ray would grow up to be a chef or work in food service. How right that man was!

Ray started out selling paper drinking cups. Then, he met a man who had invented a machine that could mix five milkshakes at a time. It was called a Multimixer.

The inventor, Earl Prince, wanted to buy truck loads of paper cups for his milkshakes.

Prince talked Ray into selling his mixers. Ray agreed enthusiatically, and he couldn't wait to sell the machine to every soda fountain, drug store and five-and-dime snack counter. He saw a double dip: the more milkshakes those snack shops sold, the more paper cups they'd buy!

Ray became the exclusive agent to sell Multimixers in the United States. And one day, selling his milkshake machines in California, he discovered a little drive-in restaurant.

The beginning of an empire

The year was 1954, and the little restaurant was called McDonald's.

That name made sense. The hamburger stop was owned by two brothers, Richard and Maurice McDonald. Besides hamburgers, the McDonalds sold cheeseburgers, French fries, Cokes and shakes. They kept the menu small and the prices cheap. Hamburgers cost 15 cents. Milkshakes cost 20 cents.

The McDonalds tried to prepare their food quickly so that customers didn't have to wait long to eat. "Our whole concept was based on speed, lower prices and volume," Mr. McDonald was quoted in *Grinding it Out*. The McDonald brothers expanded their little chain until they owned nearly a dozen restaurants.

Ray Kroc started to think "Super Size." Hmm. If he could turn McDonald's into a national chain, imagine all the Multimixers and paper cups he could sell!

Ray always did think big. "If you think about building a little business, that is what you will build," Ray wrote in his book. "But if you can imagine a giant marketing organization, you can make it happen!"

And Ray never doubted himself, not for a second. He never paid any attention to his aches or pains either. Ray suffered from diabetes and arthritis. He had already had his gall bladder and most of his thyroid removed. But Ray never gave in to his physical ailments. He didn't fret about his problems, either. He swept them out of his mind so he could get a good night's sleep and tackle things in the morning.

In that same year, Ray made a deal with the McDonald brothers to sell restaurant franchises. Then, in 1961, at the age of 59, Ray bought out the McDonald brothers for $2.7 million. Everyone laughed at Ray because $2.7 million was a huge amount of money to spend on a bunch of hamburger stands that sold 15-cent hamburgers.

A vision that paid off ... big

Ray didn't have the $2.7 million he needed in the bank, so he mortgaged his house and took out loans. With all the interest that accrued, buying McDonald's ended up costing Ray nearly five times that!

Ah, but it ended up being a bargain, just as Ray had faith it would.

After all, 96 percent of all Americans have eaten at a McDonald's restaurant at least once in their lives. And even way back in 1983, the year before Ray died, McDonald's total sales amounted to over $8 billion.

But Ray was just about the only person who believed that he was making the right move back in 1961. He didn't get much support from anyone, especially his first wife.

Ray encountered plenty of problems in building McDonald's, too. Still, he triumphed over every one of those problems, always determined to learn from adversity and grow stronger. As he wrote in his autobiography, "If you are willing to take big risks, and I always have been, you are bound to blow one once in a while."

Active thinkers never grow old.

As Ray's mother pointed out, Ray was a dreamer. But, he worked hard throughout his life to make his dreams come true. And, he kept on working into his 70's and 80's. Ray became president of McDonald's Corporation at 53, chairman at 66, and senior chairman at 75.

In 1984, when Ray died, McDonald's had 7,500 outlets in the U.S. and 31 other countries and territories.

All that success might be attributed to the character Ray developed based on one of his favorite sayings from Calvin Coolidge. It was this homily, and many of Ray's McDonald's executives hung a framed copy on their office walls:

> *Press On: Nothing in the world can take the place of persistence. Talent will not; nothing is more common than unsuccessful men with talent. Genius will not; unrewarded genius is almost a proverb. Education will not; the world is full of educated derelicts. Persistence and determination alone are omnipotent.*
>   *Calvin Coolidge*

Is it amazing or surprising that the man who built one of the United States' largest food services never graduated from high school or college? Here was a dreamer who combined his dreams with action. He knew that no high school or college degree would guarantee him success.

Hard work and determination would. As Ray said in his autobiography, "There's almost nothing you can't accomplish if you set your mind to it."

Chapter Eleven
David Goldstein, My Beloved Dad

My father, David Goldstein, was a hard worker and a dreamer. He would use both – his effort and vision - to become one of the most successful men I have ever met. He accomplished everything he ever wanted, perhaps because he never paid any attention to age or infirmities.

My dad started his last company at the age of 79, and continued to fly twelve-hour trips to China and Japan in search of new products for another two years. His right knee was arthritic and it wobbled when he stood, obviously hurting him. But, my father never complained. He never slowed down either. He worked full days until he died of cancer at the age of 81.

"It has always been my contention that if one does not use one's brain power, the ability to do so will be lost forever," my father said.

So he used his brain power right to the end. Maybe it came from having been born on the poor side of the tracks in our hometown of Rochester, N.Y. That just made my father all the more determined to achieve. His success didn't come easily, and his life was full of ups and downs. It is how my father responded to his misfortunes that is most inspirational to me. When someone slammed one door in his face, he tried his key in another lock. In doing so, he uncovered new staircases to success.

Born without privilege ... privilege hard-earned

My father's parents were Polish immigrants with no money to send my father or his two brothers to college. So my father sold newspapers and saved. At 17, my father sold enough newspapers to earn a Newspaper Boys' Association trip to the White House to shake hands with President Hoover.

After high school, my father didn't have enough money to go to college full time. So he worked a year and studied a year at the University of Rochester Institute of Optics. When he graduated as an optical engineer and found that none of the big Rochester firms would hire him because he was Jewish, he decided to start a business of his own.

In 1946, at the age of 32, my father started his first company – Elgeet Optical Company – with two other partners. He designed the camera lens that flew into space on the first weather satellite, Tiros 1. (That satellite now hangs in the Smithsonian Air and Space Museum.) My father also designed the camera lens inside the first AT&T picture phone displayed at the 1964 World's Fair.

When Elgeet was forced into bankruptcy in 1967, my father vowed to start over, this time without any partners or stock. He was 53, with two children in college and six more at home. Age didn't daunt him. Neither did the fear of failure.

My father could have told himself, "I've got a family to support and a mortgage to pay. I need a steady paycheck each week. I've got to go to work." He had more faith in himself than that. He enlisted the help of my mother, who supported him by going back to work. He sought the help of his children, too. My oldest brother and sister each took out loans to pay their college tuitions. Another brother bagged groceries in town so we would have money for food. "The next company will be even bigger and better," my father would say.

"Misfortune is no reason to complain."

Unfortunately, going through a bankruptcy was just the beginning of my father's misfortunes that year. Rochester winters are brutal, and my father skidded on the ice one day while driving. He broke his leg, and then cracked a couple of ribs when he slipped in the shower with his cast on. My father never complained, though. He didn't ever get angry at his partners or shareholders, either. What an example he set for all of us! Losers are sore and bitter. But, winners turn setbacks into new opportunities.

"After the bankruptcy, he never looked back or wasted time feeling sorry for himself," my sister Jackie has said. "He looked ahead to tomorrow as a new day and plunged forward with new ideas and a plan for starting over."

My father's new company became known as Navitar. He designed Navitar lenses for Kodak slide projectors, especially for the multi-screen productions popular in the 1970's. In 1991, when he was 76, my father sold Navitar to me and my brother Julian. We gave him an honorary title – Chairman of the Board – and he could have retired with plenty of money in the bank. But my father was bored. He decided to build yet another business, this time importing medical diagnostic instruments from China. By November of 1995, his slow-moving leukemia turned into a raging cancer throughout his chest. My father never lost hope, though. He wanted to endure one more round of chemotherapy so he could get better and go back to work. Unfortunately, my father died in 1996. Who knows what he would have gone on to accomplish if death hadn't stopped him.

My father stumbled in the workplace many times, but he kept going. That was his greatest strength – the ability to pick himself up after a fall and not think himself a failure. Okay, so maybe today he faltered. Tomorrow he'd succeed. "You can't just wish for success. You have to work for it," he said.

"Try a little harder."

Back when he was a youngster, when my father would complain to his mother that he was trying as hard as he could, she showed no sympathy. "Nu," my father's mother commented in Yiddish, "then try a little harder."

My father did. He could have written a list for all of us to follow no matter what dream we're chasing and no matter what age: set goals and work to achieve them every day. It's one thing to dream the dream; it's another to get off the couch. Try different methods, too. As my father said, "You have to have enough horses in the race so that one will reach the finish line." In other words, don't rely on any one person or thing to help you succeed.

My father taught me that failure doesn't come from falling short of the goal line. Failure comes from not having the courage to try again next time. He taught me not to give up, and to believe that one day I could achieve whatever I envisioned.

My father sent this poem to my sister Darice in college. He said it was his favorite:

The road to success is steep, my dear.
The top of the goal is high.
Faith alone will bring you there.
Faith which cannot die.

My father died a champ. Until the very moment he left this world, I don't think he ever felt he had missed out on anything or that he had one last goal he wanted to accomplish.

I was with my father the last few months of his life, and one day toward the end he said this to me: "I have achieved everything in this world that I have ever wanted. I have done everything in the world that I have ever wanted. So when it is time to get off the train, I have no regrets. I have lived a good life."

We should all be so lucky!

Chapter Twelve
Reverend Dr. Hillary Gaston, The Lord's Servant

The Rev. Dr. Hillary Gaston once served the army, the police, and the postal service. But, when he was a little boy, Rev. Gaston learned that he was really called to serve God.

"Believe it or not, I had an experience when I was seven or eight," the African-American president of the New York Theological Seminary said in his office, across from the towering white spirals of Riverside Church in Manhattan. He was wearing a navy-blue suit and red tie in his Morningside Heights office, just blocks from where he grew up in Harlem. "I remember getting up at 2 or 3 o'clock in the morning, like somebody woke me up. And there was a white figure who had come to say, `You will be my spokesperson to your people.' And I ran to my mother, and I said, `Mama, Mama, Jesus just talked to me.'"

Hillary Gaston didn't live in a very big apartment in Harlem, and Mrs. Gaston sat up in bed and watched. "The figure was still there, and he went out the kitchen window," Rev. Gaston recalled. "She saw him, too."

Rev. Gaston didn't know what all that meant, and his mother didn't either. She told her son that he'd grow up to find out.

He did, too. But, like the other remarkable individuals in this book, Rev. Gaston couldn't find the courage to listen to his heart – and serve his people – until much later in his life.

Rev. Gaston became a pastor in 1990, at the age of 43. A dozen years later, at 55, he became president of the seminary, one of the largest in New York City. He is only the second African-American president in the history of the 104-year-old institution, which educates clergy and lay people for urban ministry. Over 90 percent of its students are African-American, Asian or Hispanic.

Destined to spread God's word

Although he became a religious leader much later on in life, Rev. Gaston knew from an early age that he was meant to share God's words with his old Harlem community. But Dr. Gaston didn't feel worthy of being a minister or preaching to anybody at first. He fooled around with girls, got one pregnant, and married her. He served the country as a soldier in Vietnam. After the Vietnam War he returned and became a police officer in Baltimore. At night, he attended classes at the University of Baltimore. He graduated with a B.S. degree in accounting.

"I was living a normal life," Rev. Gaston recalled, "and when you look at the people who are ministers,

I didn't see God using someone like me."

Or maybe it was the other way around. Maybe God used people exactly like him, because Rev. Gaston grew up with not much more than faith. He was the second youngest of fourteen children and slept in a queen-sized bed with seven siblings in an apartment not a whole lot bigger than his present fourth-floor office overlooking the Hudson River – four children at the top of the bed, and four at the bottom.

"I never slept in a bed by myself until I went to college," he said. "I thought smelling feet was normal."

His father, William Gaston, Sr., had a third-grade education and fixed irons, toasters and TV's. His mother, Ethel Mae, became a domestic after ninth grade. Mr. and Mrs. Gaston couldn't give much to their children, but what they did give them was this: they taught them that if they believed in God and got a good education, there was nothing in the world their children couldn't do.

The Gastons were regular church-goers, and young Hillary grew up singing the Gospel side-by-side with them in their pew.

"Lord, I'll go where you want me to go. I'll be what you want me to be."

Hillary Gaston first won acclaim as a track star.

He was a sprinter in grade school, when there was a little more hair on his head and a little less girth around the middle. When he was in the sixth grade at P.S. 24, he won the 100-yard dash in a meet on Randall's Island.

He was disqualified because he was barefoot.

"Sneakers or shoes, we couldn't afford them," he shrugged.

The track meet officials didn't understand, and Rev. Gaston said he was too ashamed to say anything. Besides, his parents always taught him to respect people in authority.

But Rev. Gaston never forgot that incident. He said it didn't let it defeat him either. "I said, this won't happen again. I'm not going to make life better for me, I'm going to make it better for other people, too. When I get to a point where I can make a difference, I will."

God has a way of making us keep our promises, too, he said.

And the Rev. Dr. Gaston kept his promise and continues to make it better for other people every day. While in Vietnam, he gave his G.I. rations away to children after watching them scavenge through the soldiers' garbage. He began seeing for the first time that poor people in the U.S. were a heap better off than poor people in the rest of the world. "I wanted to help," he said. "I began to understand that poverty is relative."

When he was a police officer, he would go on domestic violence calls and try to get the women who were beaten by their husbands to leave. He would practice the foundation of all Judeo-Christian religion – to do unto others as he would want them to do unto him. People were his passion. He loved them and taught them to love themselves.

His sergeant chewed him out, saying he spent too much time with people. "If you wanted to be a social worker, why don't you become a social worker," the sergeant barked.

"Serving God is not just on Sunday."

Rev. Gaston didn't know he was already following his life's calling, ministering to people as best he could. He didn't think he could attend a seminary until after he retired, but he was actually preaching to the people in the vineyards the way his Jesus had. For Rev. Gaston, the vineyards became the street or the living rooms of poor people's homes.

Years later, sitting in his office, he marveled that "Everything we do is sacred. Serving God is not just on Sunday. It's a 24/7 experience, in every walk of life regardless of what your profession is. Whatever vocation God has called you to, that is your ministry." And, at the time, "my career in law enforcement, that was my ministry."

After law enforcement, Rev. Gaston became a federal agent for the Postal Service in Charlotte, N.C. He was eight years away from retirement and a full pension when he had another dream. This time, the dream told him that a brother would die and that he would return home.

"Wow, God, you're making it plain," he thought.

Rev. Gaston's brother did die of a heart attack a year later, and the future minister did move back home. "The desire to get my education and help people always stayed there," he said.

He enrolled at a night program at the Theological Seminary, and graduated with a Master of Divinity degree in 1986. In 1990, he was offered a job as pastor of the Parkchester Baptist Church in Bronx, N.Y.

The trouble was, as a pastor, he would only earn half of the salary that he had earned with the Postal Service. Rev. Gaston's wife was furious. She told him he'd downsized. "I didn't meet you as a minister," she said. Although the couple had two children, she finally left him a few years later. She took with her a huge chunk of their combined income because she was a psychiatric social worker.

The way out of no way

What was he doing, Rev. Gaston wondered? In that sacrificial leap of faith, he remembered what he had learned in church growing up. God is able to make a way out of no way, and to make a crooked way straight.

Rev. Gaston's first church congregation were primarily African-American, Hispanic, and Caribbean, yet the management structure of the church was still white. Rev. Gaston was the first "pastor of color," as he put it. His parents had taught him that whatever he did, though, he should try to be the best.

At first, only 50 or 60 parishioners sat down to listen to the new black minister on Sunday. But, when they heard this warm-hearted, compassionate man speak, they told their friends. Word of mouth spread, and soon there were 300 people sitting in the pews in front of him. It became a true community church.

During the week, Rev. Gaston taught history at nearby Samuel Gompers High School in the Bronx. He taught his students to reach for success, that failure was not an option, and that "no" was an unacceptable word.

Rev. Gaston will tell you about his mother, who went back to school when she was 74 and graduated. "She had always said she was determined to get her high school degree," he said. "That is the line I come from."

Rev. Gaston likes to quote the late Rev. Martin Luther King: "A dream deferred is not a dream denied."

And he has a few words of advice for others who

still have a dream. "Do it," he said. "Don't wish it. Do it, because God still makes a way out of no way."

Chapter Thirteen
Mike Milken, Determined Philanthropist

Michael Milken was 26 when he found his life's passion. It was back in 1972, when he learned his wife's mother had cancer. Mike's passion, it turns out, was to find a cure.

Unfortunately, Mike was to lose his mother-in-law, father, and five other relatives to that deadly disease. And while Mike was a lot younger than the other people in this book when he threw himself into his quest, his passion might help you live longer.

Cancer is, after all, the second leading killer in the United States. Its victims tend to be older, too. As the American Cancer Society reports, about 77 percent of all cancer patients are diagnosed when they're 55 or older. If you're over 55, that could be you. One in two men will develop cancer in the U.S. One in three women will suffer, too.

The defining statistic: people who die from cancer could have lived an average of 15 years more if they hadn't had the disease. Fifteen more years beside loved ones. Fifteen more years to live out dreams.

Back in the year 1900, one in five babies wouldn't live to the age of five. In the 21st century we have antibiotics and vaccines that could save them. But, sadly, today's babies aren't much better off. Today, one in every five babies is still expected to die, but this time of cancer.

As Mike Milken says, "Our children face a greater chance of dying from cancer than our grandparents. We can sit back and wait for a cure in a generation or two, losing at least another ten to twenty million more American mothers, fathers, children, co-workers and friends. Or we can mobilize and find a cure now."

Mike's mother-in-law died of breast cancer while he was working in Manhattan for his brokerage house, Drexel Burnham Lambert. And, not long after she was diagnosed with cancer, Mike suffered a second blow. He learned that his father had malignant melanoma. This time, Mike didn't want to be on the other side of the country while someone he loved was dying.

Mike moved his entire office to Los Angeles so that he could be closer to his father and help in any way he could. Unfortunately, there was not much more Mike could do to save his father than he could to save his wife's mother.

The controversial but dedicated philanthropist

Around this time, Mike became one of America's most fervent philanthropists. His mission was to help people find cures for cancer and other terrible diseases. In 1982, Mike and his brother turned his philanthropy into an official organization through the founding of the Milken Family Foundation.

Then, in 1993 – following a controversial sentence for securities fraud – Mike became a cancer victim, too. He was diagnosed with advanced prostate cancer, and doctors gave him 12 to 18 more months to live.

Mike didn't accept that prognosis or give up. He maintained an upbeat attitude, which probably saved his life.

Mike decided to fight back. First, he learned all he could about prostate cancer. He thought he might have a better chance of surviving the disease if he became a vegetarian, so he gave up eating burgers and fries. Soon, his diet consisted of soy shakes, vegetables and other healthy ingredients. To relax himself and stay positive, Mike turned to meditation and yoga. He remodeled his kitchen and library in light-colored pine. He installed a soothing fountain outside his window, and planted honeysuckle and jasmine in the garden to give it a joyful scent.

Mike reached out to help others, too. He didn't want to sit back and wait for a cure. He wanted to help find one.

To do that, Mike Milken founded the Prostate Cancer Foundation, which has raised over $200 million to find new drugs and treatments for that disease. It has become the largest philanthropic source of funds for prostate cancer research. Mike's Foundation simplified and speeded up the grant-writing process, making it possible for one hundred grants to be awarded and eighty new treatments tested. Spending on prostate cancer research increased twenty times, from $27 million in 1993 to $550 million in 2003. As a result, the number of men over age 50 dying of prostate cancer each year has dropped dramatically since 1992: a 28 percent decline in fewer than ten years. (Prostate cancer is the only cancer for which deaths have declined.)

More than a survivor, an advocate

Michael Milken did survive prostate cancer. He has lived to help others survive. He organized the first National Cancer Summit, in 1995, where he proposed a ten-point action plan to speed up the war on cancer. For instance, Mike noted that more than 90 percent of all cancer deaths occur outside the U.S., and that the U.S. needed to consolidate its efforts with these other countries to find a cure. It didn't make sense to duplicate efforts.

Some of Mike's logical proposals were adopted by the National Institutes of Health. And, Mike went on to found the Center for Accelerating Medical Solutions (CAMS). Mike is convinced that we have the talent and resources in the world to cure major diseases like cancer *in our lifetime.* CAMS is a non-profit think tank, dedicated to shortening the time it takes to find cures and improving treatment for the most deadly diseases. CAMS works to recruit the brightest students to cancer research, coordinate world resources, eliminate unnecessary government regulation, increase the number of patients in clinical trials, and get new drugs out to patients faster. (Unfortunately, with current government regulations, it often takes 10 to 15 years for new drugs to be approved.)

According to Mike Milken, we all need to fight the war on cancer ... not only for ourselves, but for our children and future generations.

With all his humanitarian work on behalf of cancer research, it is no wonder that Mike has been praised by scientists, scholars and journalists alike. In the magazine *Vanity Fair*, Dominick Dunne wrote that one doctor told him that Mike "had advanced the study of the disease by 40 years." *Business Week* wrote that Mike "has done more to advance the cause than anyone." And *U.S. News & World Report* said, "The work is making a difference."

And that is why Mike Milken has a chapter in this book. Mike's positive attitude and passion, finding a cure for cancer, probably saved his life and can possibly help save yours. His example is a lesson to everyone.

Maybe we should all follow Mike's example and

get involved in helping to find a cure. The more people who join in the fight, the greater the chances for all of us to live out our dreams.

In his 1995 speech to the National Cancer Summit, Mike recalled John F. Kennedy's 1961 challenge to the American people. He said that eight million cancer survivors in the United States, survivors just like him, were joining millions of other survivors around the world and asking what they could do to help save their lives and the lives of future generations.

One man like Mike made a difference. And, if we all take a proactive approach the way he did, our families and we might benefit one day, too.

(For further information on Mike Milken's cancer fighting efforts, see www.mikemilken.com)

Chapter Fourteen
Bunny Voss, A Reverend After A 40-Year Quest

Talking to Reverend Margaret "Bunny" Voss is like drinking a strong cup of espresso. Your heart is racing and you feel like you could take on the world!

At any age.

Bunny is determined to make the most out of every day and to help others do the same.

She is an 82-year-old Congregational minister and psychotherapist. She is also on the board of the Great Lakes Center for Sages in Grand Rapids, Mich. The center teaches elderly people that they are sages with precious wisdom to share. As Bunny says to the crinkly set, "You're not old, you're rich!"

After all, that's how Bunny views herself. "I have 82 years of life experience," she says.

Unfortunately, Bunny does not think American culture views older people this way or values them. She said that all you have to do is watch TV.

"It is a national trend where people are living healthier, longer lives yet we are in a very strong youth culture," Bunny said. "We are losing as a culture all the wisdom and experience of the older population."

The present youth culture isn't benefiting from the wisdom and experience of its older citizens. "In our society, there is so much emphasis on youth," Bunny told a reporter from the *Grand Rapids Press*. "But, when you're older, you have worth. You have dignity. ...You can gain a sense of peace about aging."

You can also grow. Bunny believes that aging does not have to be a time of shriveling, and that older people can still learn and blossom.

A formidable force!

The optimism and gentle encouragement are part of her nature. Bunny's been nurturing people throughout her life as a mother, minister, college dean and psychotherapist.

"I've been blessed with long life and with energy," she said.

And how. Bunny started off being a minister, although it took her a while. For when Bunny was growing up in Chelmsford, Mass. in the 1920's and 30's, women ministers were about as common as women doctors.

There weren't many. "They weren't encouraging the ordination of women back then," she said.

Bunny took seminary classes anyway, although she used them to become a religious education director. She left ministering to her husband, who was also a professor, and focused on raising their three adopted children. Then, she started working at a local university in Grand Rapids, becoming the first female dean of students at Davenport College. She would have kept on working into her 70's if the university hadn't forced her to retire at 65.

Bunny didn't want to pack up her office, but she made the most of the departure. After leaving the university, she used the opportunity to grow in a different direction. She felt that her later years could be just as meaningful, productive, and joyous as the earlier ones.

So could the second half of your life.

She didn't want to retire. She knew from talking with others that retirement wasn't all it was cracked up to be. "You talk to a few retired people and find that after a year of golf or swimming or golf and bridge they begin to realize that they still have a lot to offer and where do they offer it?" she said.

"From Age-ing to Sage-ing"

In Bunny's case, she became a private psychotherapist. Then, in 1999, she helped found the Great Lakes Center for Sages. It all started when she was thumbing through the bookshelf in her local bookstore and one particular book happened to fall at her feet. It was called "From Age-ing to Sage-ing: A Profound New Vision of Growing Older" by Zalman Schachter-Shalomi and Ronald S. Miller.

Bunny thought it was a profound vision from above. She picked up the book and bought it. She thought there was a divine reason that that book dropped into her life.

The Sage-ing movement was founded by Rabbi Zalman Schachter-Shalomi, who started the Spiritual Eldering Institute in Boulder, Colo. back in 1989. The institute believes that the elders of a community should be valued for the wisdom they have to share, and that they should share that wisdom – that inner sage – with the people around them by becoming leaders, mentors and healers in their community.

"The idea is to move from aging – the aching joints, the frail bodies – to a saging level of respect, sharing wisdom, speaking out," Bunny told Terri Finch Hamilton of the *Grand Rapids Press*.

Bunny flew out to Boulder to learn how to become a spiritual leader. Later, she helped found the Great Lakes Center. Soon, it was offering workshops and classes in the art of sage-ing.

Bunny believes that our society is preoccupied with youth and doesn't care about what older people have to offer. She wants to help change that and help elderly people feel a sense of pride in what they've gained along with those wrinkles. Her center offers 2-hour classes in dusting off dreams, harvesting lives, becoming a sage, forgiveness, and living with wonder. There is also a class on "The Heart Has No

Wrinkles," or sex education for the senior set. The center also sponsors a "Circle of Sages" - a monthly discussion group about the journey toward wise aging. There are classes on passing on one's legacy, too.

The Center is a partnership between Grand Rapids Community College, a local health center, and a church - or mind, body and soul. The three partners of the Great Lakes Center for Sages represent the triangle of the sage-ing movement. Bunny believes that working on one's mind, body and soul is the best way to enjoy life.

Bunny believes that all of us were born with a divine spark, or sage. "I think we have to recognize and develop a grateful heart for the fact that there is a spark or bit of the divine in every human being," she said. We should be grateful for the divine spark within us and open to the opportunities to come.

"Every single one of us lives in a community, and with that divine power and divine wisdom and that gratitude we can change and grow, and we do things that are surprising as we continue to grow," she said.

Bunny thinks there's nothing stopping us from doing anything we want later in life, and that it may be the perfect time to make a dream come true. Raising a family, she said, is hard. But, "after your children are grown, those responsibilities are no longer there and you have that freedom and you get more energy as you follow your dream, and why not?"

Although most men and women cringe at the thought of turning 40, 50, or 60, Bunny helps them embrace each new aging milestone. She believes that there is a richness still ahead, despite what others fear.

The Center is the only one of its kind in Michigan and has served more than a thousand people in its workshops. Bunny hopes it can expand and train new leaders, too.

Looking back at her own life, Bunny feels it has been like a book, with each chapter rich and full. And, Bunny looks at her present life as a chance to share her bounty with others.

She has plenty of advice for older men and women. For instance, don't stop at one thing. Keep going. Every failure is an opportunity to learn, and every one can teach you something.

Chapter Fifteen
Rosalind Klein, Master Gardener

Rosalind Klein found her own fountain of youth in a surprising place. Right in her back yard.

My aunt, who is now 85, started gardening during World War II. After all, it was the patriotic thing to do. Americans were encouraged to plant fruits and vegetables so the country would not have a shortage of food. The gardens were called victory gardens, and they were planted in backyards and on rooftops across the country. Rosalind watched her father plant three fruit trees in the backyard. Later, she watched her husband Stanley grow vegetables. My aunt grew to love planting flower beds and vegetables.

Rosalind kept improving her skills over time and as recently as May 2004, she completed the Master Gardener program from Cornell University. With her newest credentials, she became a certified master gardener, master judge, and accredited landscape critic.

Little did my aunt know that gardening would keep her young.

Through the years, my aunt has worked out in her garden every chance she gets. Her gardens have been featured on garden club tours. And, from all that tilling the soil and yanking out weeds, my aunt has the energy of someone 30 years younger. She doesn't suffer from osteoporosis. She doesn't take vitamins, antidepressants or any kind of medication either. She is, moreover, a breast cancer survivor.

So what's Rosalind's secret? Gardening.

What Rosalind's life teaches us is that gardening is more than a hobby. It's great exercise, too. It is something that anyone can do from the age of 3 or 4 to over 100. Rosalind has 2.7 acres of gardens around her house, from curved flower beds to a large square vegetable plot. She takes care of every inch of landscaping herself. She rakes, plants trees, trims shrubs, pulls weeds, and composts herself. She digs holes and moves stones. The only thing she doesn't do? Cut the grass.

A challenging and worthwhile workout

Aunt Rosalind gets a great whole-body workout without the bodily stress. She incorporates many essentials of exercise programs like stretching, aerobics and weight lifting. All that digging, spading, raking, tilling and hoeing is great aerobic exercise without having to run off to the gym or into the street! Plus, Rosalind uses up almost the same calories as she would on a treadmill, exercise bike, or leisurely jog. According to the National Gardening Association (www.nationalgardening.com), a 180-pound person will burn up 162 calories during 30 minutes of raking. Planting trees, weeding, or trimming shrubs for a half hour will use up another 182 calories. Finally, laying sod for 30 minutes will use up 202 calories, and turning compost will eat up a whopping 250!

With all the time she spends in the garden, Rosalind does not go out for other forms of exercise. She feels that her work in the garden is a well rounded workout in itself. Not to mention her housework.

Rosalind isn't a smoker, and she stays healthy by preparing well-rounded meals with many of the fruits and vegetables she grows. She doesn't supplement her diet with vitamins because she feels she already gets enough vitamins from the food she eats. She particularly likes the fruits and vegetables from her garden because they are all organic. She doesn't use any pesticides, and Rosalind believes that bending over in her garden may be just what it takes to keep osteoporosis away. She may be right, too. According to a 2000 University of Arkansas study, yard work was extremely helpful in preventing osteoporosis in women age 50 and older.

Although she was born in 1919, long before the baby boomers, Rosalind is like them in that she refuses to accept the fact that she's getting older. "When I say that I am 85, I just don't believe it," she said. Looking at her, no one else can believe it, either.

Accentuating the positives

Rosalind believes in God and that everything happens for the best. Her positive attitude is just one of her secrets to staying young. Her husband Stanley has Parkinson's disease, but Rosalind looks on the bright side of that, too. She counts her blessings and considers herself lucky. After all, she still has her husband. They still live at home and not in a nursing home, and both of them can still do many things.

If a loved one passes away, and a few have, Rosalind finds a silver lining in that, too. She thinks it's a chance to go back to school, learn something new, or become closer with other family members. After losing her beloved sister Evelyn, Rosalind started taking gardening classes at Cornell University. She completed a master gardener program in May 2004. She is now a master judge, and accredited landscape critic, along with a master gardener.

Rosalind knows that time doesn't go on forever. Somewhere along the way, life is going to come to a screeching halt. That is all the more reason for people to go after their dreams and goals today. And, Rosalind is living her dream of a happy and healthy life.

Rosalind's believes that a lot of people get sick because they have nothing else to do but be sick. She says that if she wanted to sit around and think about how tired she was, then she would feel tired and depressed. Rosalind believes that no one should sit around feeling sorry for themselves or that they're not fulfilled. She says they can try her passion, gardening, or a dozen other hobbies. Towns and community schools across the country offer classes for everyone from desk top publishing to recovering chairs.

According to Rosalind, "If you want to do something, just get up and do it. All you have to do is reach out." Just get off your duff, she says.

For those who want to try their hand at gardening and unlock some of Rosalind's fountain of youth secrets, there are federated garden clubs from New York to California, willing and ready to take anybody. So before you spend good money on the latest flab-blaster or diet pills, why not try gardening? Invest in a good pair of gardening gloves and give gardening a try!

Chapter Sixteen
The Million Dollar Man – The Ernie Harwell Story

You're never too old to get a 10-year $1,000,000 contract. Ernie Harwell has proven that.

Ernie Harwell always loved baseball. As a kid, he'd listen to the World Series on the radio in the basement of his Georgia home. The game would be tied, the bases loaded, and there would be Ernie – hanging on to every pitch.

Ernie was hooked. He wanted to grow up, sit in a radio booth, and describe the games, too. Red Barber and Mel Allen were his heroes. He would pretend he was each of them, depending on who was announcing the play-by-play that day.

The trouble was, Ernie couldn't talk very well. He was tongue-tied, he stuttered, and other kids made fun of him. His speech was so bad his parents hired speech teachers, even though they really couldn't afford them.

Where there's a will...

Did Ernie overcome his speech difficulties? Well, you decide. He went on to broadcast games for 48 years, from 1943 to 1991. In 1948, he told Brooklyn

Dodger fans about the rookie Jackie Robinson. In 1951, he described the debut of Willie Mays for the New York Giants. He took a turn in the Baltimore Orioles' booth before moving to the Tigers in 1960.

Ernie was warm, he was funny, and he talked to listeners as though they were friends. Ernie called each play with the proper voice pitch, and fans loved to hear him say "loooong gone!"

In 1990, Ernie Harwell was still doing what he loved up in the radio booth when the Detroit Tigers told him to turn off the mike. Ernie was 72, and the Tiger organization thought he was too old to keep on announcing their games on radio and television. The hair was white and the face was wrinkled, regardless that the reason for those creases was a good-natured smile.

"In December of 1990, the Tiger organization called me in and said that they wanted me to work one more year and they were going to replace me," Ernie said.

Yet, Ernie didn't feel old. Day after day, he traveled with the young ball players on the Tiger bus. He narrated the games at night, boarded the bus again to the next city, and climbed back in the announcer's booth with high enthusiasm the next day. "I could keep up with the young guys. It didn't bother me," he said.

Ernie was in great shape. It was because he took care of himself. He walked every day and jumped rope

300 times a day, too. Plus, he lifted weights. He wanted to keep on working, chatting to the fans he loved. He couldn't imagine any greater job in the world. Ernie wasn't ready to retire. "I thought that I was still doing the job as well as I had," he said.

The fans have a say-so!

Ready or not, the Tigers called Ernie "out" after 8,500 television and radio broadcasts. In all those years, Ernie had missed just two games. "Neither one because of health," he made it clear.

But now, Ernie was like a 70-year-old judge facing mandatory retirement. He had to make way for ducklings. Ernie was hurt, but he wasn't bitter. He knew everyone had to move on eventually.

Fans were not as forgiving, though. They revolted, slapping angry bumper stickers on their cars. They were angry that they would no longer hear that familiar Georgia drawl cracking them up during a tense moment. A typical Ernie on-the-air crack was: "Something's got to break loose, like the fat lady's girdle."

Luckily for both Ernie and the fans, new Tigers owner Mike Illitch rehired Ernie in August 1992 when he bought the team. Ernie was grateful for the chance to get back in the booth the following year. Then, *ten years later*, in 2002, Ernie himself decided that the time was right for him to get up from the mike.

"I wanted to go out while my game was still okay," he said.

The Tigers came up with a farewell tribute and called it Ernie Harwell Day. On September 29, 2002, Ernie called his last game and made a speech. "One of the highlights of my career, one of the things I'm most grateful for, is that when Mike Illitch bought the Tigers, he brought me back to be the announcer," Ernie said at Comerica Park. He was overcome by the sight of his statue now greeting fans at the main entrance to the park. The statue showed Ernie was holding a microphone, just like he loved to do.

A new career at 84!

Blue Cross Blue Shield (BCBS) was sponsoring that game, and Ernie's agent was on the field that day. "My agent was talking to one of the executives of BCBS about me and they said maybe we can use this guy as a spokesman. That is how it got started," Ernie said.

Maybe it wasn't time to retire Ernie's number just yet. Blue Cross Blue Shield wanted Ernie to represent them in newspaper and magazine ads, in speeches, and in broadcast commercials.

Ernie had come a long way from having a speech impediment. Now, at the age of 84, he was signing a

$1,000,000 ten-year contract with an option for another ten. Imagine. Ernie could work until he was 94 or 104!

Ernie didn't mind trying out a new career. "As we get older, we tend to want to stay in our comfort zone a little too long," Ernie said. "It's good to have something that will press you out of that comfort zone. I think it is nice to do something new once in a while." What a delightful understatement.

Ernie is glad to skip retirement and keep working. "You have to stay active both physically and mentally," he said. "I think it's good for everybody to do things and get away from the TV and sitting around the sofa all the time. It's good to branch out once in a while and not just stay in your same job. Try something new and see how it goes."

Ernie has become not only a spokesman for Blue Cross Blue Shield but also for older people everywhere. He is a devout Christian with a good heart. "I'm trying to help people. I am trying to get a message out," he says. "You have to take care of yourself. You can't overextend yourself. You have to reverse the trends of obesity and inactivity."

Ernie has been working all his life and doesn't mind continuing. He still enjoys life and looks forward to each new day. "I grew up in the Depression," he said. "When I was a kid, I sold magazines, Christmas cards, things people would want to buy. Then I worked on the paper in high school for six years. I did magazine writing. I've always worked. I don't mind working at all. I enjoy it."

Ernie's last call for the Tigers back in 2002 was simple. "Swing and a miss," he said when the first baseman struck out.

Ernie never struck out. He keeps on swinging, too.

Chapter Seventeen
Jack McKeon, World Series Winner

Even at 72, Jack McKeon didn't think he was old. "You're as old as you feel," the Florida Marlins team manager said. "Age is just a number." And McKeon's number was red hot during the 2003 baseball season.

That year, McKeon quit retirement to become the oldest manager ever to win a World Series. End of story? Hardly.

In five months, McKeon had turned a losing team, and himself, into a winner. The Marlins started out 16-22 in the season and bloomed late.

Just like McKeon.

Jack was a gruff old cigar-smoking manager who was used to getting dumped mid-season by some big league team. McKeon had been fired four times in the major leagues, and he'd been regarded in the baseball world as second-rate all his life. Still, at 72, McKeon didn't flinch at taking on the New York Yankees – to fulfill a lifelong dream.

He'd always wanted to win a World Series. Who wouldn't? But first, McKeon just wanted to make it to the major leagues. As a teenager, McKeon said he watched Allie Clark, another boy from his hometown of South Amboy, New Jersey, make it across the

Hudson to play two dozen games for the 1947 Yankees.

Jack McKeon started dreaming. Maybe he could make it to the pros one day, too! Of course, McKeon seemed like a dark horse in high school, since he was more apt to strike out than make it on base. Even when he eventually managed to get hired by the Pittsburgh Pirates as a catcher, McKeon realized he wasn't going to make it as a player.

Okay, I'm not a player. But...

Instead of getting down on himself, McKeon, looked around at his options. What else could he do with his favorite sport besides play?

Hey. Maybe he could manage a team.

And, manage McKeon did. In 1955, McKeon managed his first professional game in Fayetteville, N.C. It soon seemed he was striking out. In the early 1970's, he spent three years with the Kansas City Royals. Then, he was replaced. He spent three years with the Oakland Athletics and got kicked out of there. McKeon didn't manage a major league team for nine years before the Cincinnati Reds hired him.

Oops. Three years later, in 2000, the Reds let McKeon go, too. McKeon was forced to retire.

Out of work, living in North Carolina, McKeon played with his grandkids. Even in retirement, though, he couldn't stop watching baseball or smoking his cigars. He loved the game of baseball, and he felt he had learned a lot, even when he'd failed.

Jack kept in shape and exercised daily. Maybe one day he would return to the game and win that World Series. If only someone would give him one more chance.

It looked like no one would. Three years passed quietly and it looked like McKeon's baseball career was finished.

Finished? Not Yet!

During the 2003 season, the Florida Marlins weren't happy. The team was on a huge losing streak. The owner of the Marlins thought nothing of calling up McKeon as a replacement for the 61-year-old manager the owner had just fired. Besides, recycling managers and coaches to revive flailing teams seemed like the easy thing to do. After all, Hubie Brown, 70, was coaching basketball down in Memphis. Dick Vermeil, 67, was coaching football in Kansas City, and Joe Gibbs, 63, would soon be back on the Washington Redskins sidelines.

As Patrick Hruby wrote in *The Washington Times*, "Every McKeon victory cigar, every Vermeilian tear, every self-effacing Gibbsian chuckle proves you're never too old and wrinkled, let alone incontinent, to get back in the ring."

So, at 72, McKeon followed the example set by baseball managers Connie Mack (88) and Casey Stengel (75).

Truly, McKeon just wanted to have fun. And being back in the dugout was fun. McKeon was energized around the young players. Hanging around the twenty-something hotshots made him feel young again. Some of those players didn't have impressive stats, but McKeon couldn't read the fine print on the stat sheet too well anyway. McKeon listened to his gut. He believed in his players and helped them believe in themselves.

McKeon believed his team could take on anybody. And, they did. Nobody, from the sportscasters to the Las Vegas odds-makers, gave the Marlins any chance of even making the playoffs, let alone winning the pennant. But they earned a National League wild card berth. Down three games to one against the heavily-favored Chicago Cubs, they had the impossible job of beating the Cubs twice at Wrigley Field while facing two of the best pitchers in baseball.

The wily Jack McKeon went with his hunches. As usual, they were unconventional. The Marlins pitching coach, Wayne Rosenthal, encapsulated McKeon's strategies: "Every move that guy wants to do works."

You know the result. He took a losing team, sent them out against impossible odds, first won the National League race and then had his team beat giants like the Yankees. In the World Series, his team, originally down and regarded by press and fans alike as out, shut out the Bronx Bombers in game six. The Marlins came from behind and won ... just like their 72-year-old manager.

"This has always been his dream," McKeon's sister, Marge Gorczyca, told *The Newark Star-Ledger*. "I'm so happy he got a chance to live that dream."

Hey, Marge, he's still living it.

Chapter Eighteen
Seven Easy Rules For Success At 50 And Beyond

The folks in this book share a lot of common traits that begins with their positive attitude. They believe, like Jack McKeon, that they can take on the Yankees. They can win the game, sign the deal, or go back to school. And, even if they wash out at first and don't make it, they're philosophical and bounce back pretty quickly. They aren't disappointed for long!

These individuals are an inspiration for all of us. Plus, if you adopt the characteristics of these achievers, you can make your dreams come true.

Seven easy rules can get you out of the starting gate, if you're 50 or older ... or for that matter, 50 or younger. Take a look.

1. Be Positive!

No matter what happens, there's always a bright side. If it rains all summer, the lawn will be green. If you're let go from work, you have a chance to go after the job you really wanted. If your car breaks down, well, think of all the exercise you'll get running to the bus!

The glass is always half full – if you look at it right.

The people in this book always see the glass that way. I remember my mother saying time after time, "Things always turn out for the best." When my father's first company went into bankruptcy, all of us were forced to pitch in and go to work. It was good for us. We bought our own clothes and put ourselves through school. We felt good.

Meantime, my father never spent any time getting angry with the individuals or corporations who conspired against him. Or, if he did, he channeled it in a positive way – like, he'd show THEM. He'd make his next company bigger and better than the first! He did, too! My father looked forward to future opportunities. What was past was past.

After my father died, my mother didn't let her back pain, cataracts or hearing loss keep her from going to law school. Anyone else could have said, "There's no way I can keep up with those 22-year-olds!" Even when administrators suggested that she go part-time, my mother said no. She wanted to go full-time. "I can do it," she told herself.

My father and mother were both optimistic. Then again, all the people in this book are.

Grandma Moses always made the best out of life. When her fingers were too arthritic to embroider, she dabbed at some paint. And, when her husband died, she kept on painting. She felt that the spirit of her husband was with her when she painted.

Ray Kroc made plenty of bad decisions in his business career. When he did, he figured he couldn't get everything right all of the time, and there was no use getting upset over it. He believed there was nothing he couldn't accomplish if he set his mind to it. He became a billionaire in the process.

I think a positive attitude is one of the most important characteristics you can have, and I am not convinced that you're either born with it or you're not. You *can* learn to think positively, and the process starts by talking back to that nasty inner voice that says you'll never do this or that. Speak up and say, "Oh yes, I can!"

Want to gain a positive attitude? Set small goals and achieve them. With each success, your confidence builds. You'll begin to see that all things are possible, because they are!

That's what Martha de Varona used to tell her daughter, Donna. At 17, Donna brought home two gold medals in swimming from the 1960 Summer Olympics in Rome. She went on to become an ABC sportscaster. In an interview, Donna's mother recalled, , "All things are possible, I used to tell her. If you have the desire, and you've got the dream and you hang on to it, and you work hard, people along the way will help you. You can do it. It's tough, but you can do it."

George Brunstad never won a gold medal at the Olympics. That didn't make him think there wasn't a prayer he could swim across a 21-mile icy English Channel. He just kept repeating Walt Disney: "If you dream it, you can do it." Or, he'd quote Henry David Thoreau: "Go confidently in the direction of your dreams." And that's what he did.

2. Think Young!

"I don't feel old!"

Every one of the people in this book said that, over and over. George Brunstad said, "I don't know how old I feel, but it's not 69!" He kept training in the same pool as the teenagers on the Wilton Y Wahoos, the national YMCA champs. He sometimes swam more laps than the Wahoos did.

When Rosalind Klein turned 80, she went outside and did the same things she did at 20. She knelt down in her garden and started yanking the weeds. She worked until late afternoon the way she always did.

David Goldstein never thought he ought to slow down and take it easy. He saw himself as the same young salesman and deal maker he'd been fifty years ago. If his knee ached or he felt tired, he kept right on moving. He traveled overseas, well into his 80's.

Bunny Voss believes that the heart has no wrinkles. The heart knows no age, too.

3. Get Out And Mix!

Jeanette Goldstein refused to move into an assisted living center with her elderly friends. At first, she didn't want to live there because she said she'd be living in a fish bowl, with no privacy. Then, she started law school and realized that it wasn't healthy to live in a retirement home. The reason wasn't privacy. It was just that everyone was ... old and retired!

Jeanette said it was healthier to be around young people, and that absolutely was true in her case. Being in law school energized Jeanette and inspired her to keep up with the people in her class. The young people Jeanette met at law school were excited about the future. That made her excited, too, and their bright outlook on life rubbed off on her. Not that Jeanette had ever been a gloomy person, but it's hard to be in a room full of bouncing electrons and not get hit with that energy!

None of the people interviewed for this book live in old age homes or retirement communities. Not one. They enjoy living in a mixed community where they still walk among young people. Seeing young people boosts their spirits.

You should surround yourself with young people, too. Go to the gym where they hang out and walk on the treadmill besides them. Lift a few weights like they do. Take an exercise class with the 20- and 30-

year-olds. You'll be amazed at how energetic you'll feel around people half your age. You'll feel more their age than yours!

4. Be Persistent!

If there is something you want to do, don't let anyone talk you out of it. Dr. Gail Fredericks was told she'd never get admitted to medical school and that even if she did, she'd never become a doctor.
Well, she did.

Gail didn't get discouraged or give up when all the admissions nay-sayers spoke. She just kept on asking questions – like, what classes did she need to take? Then, she signed up for those courses, one by one.

None of the people in this book were quitters. Quite the contrary. They were persistent and insisted that they could do whatever it was they wanted to do. They overcame any obstacles in order to make the slam-dunk.

Taking the law school entrance exam was Jeanette Goldstein's biggest hurdle, but she overcame it. She took the LSAT preparation course, and now she's on to the bar review classes so she can practice law after graduation. Her determination enabled her to stick with it until she succeeded.

Rev. Dr. Hillary Gaston started preaching in a near-empty church. He didn't give up, though. He reached out to the people in his community, telling his messages each Sunday until his church filled with men and women eager to hear his words. Even though Rev. Gaston's wife left him, he kept right on preaching. It was what he had wanted to do all his life.

5. Mark The Goal!

You need a goal, no matter what it is. Margaret Hagerty wanted to stop smoking. Then, she wanted to run marathons. Hillary Gaston, Sr., wanted to be a minister to the people in his community. Gail Fredericks wanted to be a doctor because she thought she could do a better job giving bad news to the sick. Jeanette Goldstein wanted to be a lawyer because she thought she could do a better job than her husband's lawyers. Mike Milken wanted to help find a cure for cancer and save lives.

Dr. Gail Fredericks said that each of us needs to find something that makes us feel like we can contribute to the universe.

With a clear purpose and a realistic objective, all these folks persevered in order to reach the goal they'd set for themselves. In the case of Mike Milken, the goal to cure cancer is saving not only *his* life but could also be helping to save all of us.

6. Go With The Flow!

Nothing turns out quite like we expected. There are always complications we could never envision. But, we can transform setbacks into opportunities. Margaret Hagerty ran marathons, but when her knee started to hurt, she dove in the pool. She didn't give up on her goal to run. She swam to keep up her endurance and she changed her goals. This one was even loftier: she'd master swimming so she could become a triathlete! She'd swim, bike and run!

Tragedy strikes all of us at one time or another. Some of us, however, are better at turning that inevitable sadness into joy. You, too, can respond positively and go with the flow.

7. Stay Active!

Not one of these individuals can be found sitting around watching television all night long. The people profiled in this book are much too busy. They're studying in the law library, or out making house calls.

It's important for both your mental health and your physical health to stay active through work or exercise. A brisk walk outside for 30 minutes can get you charged up to tackle the next step on your dream list.

Rosalind Klein looks like she cupped her hands in the fountain of youth because she digs her hands in her garden each day. Puttering in the garden all spring and summer gives her cheeks a youthful glow.

And Jeanette Goldstein? She was getting her exercise walking briskly to her law school classes. Law office next? It's her call, and you can bet she's going to make that call with all her youthful enthusiasm.

Chapter Nineteen
This Way To Your Dreams: A Step-By-Step Guide

The goal of this book is to help you reach all your goals and dreams. There's nothing like the feeling of finally achieving something you couldn't accomplish in the past and making a dream come true. The feeling is priceless!

Everyone can achieve what they want. Achievement means first desiring something, then setting that desire into a goal, then breaking down the goal into smaller parts, and voila! You're taking the first steps towards your goal. I'm quite sure you're already busy doing many things in your life. Maybe you should do a quick accounting to see if what you are doing is actually getting you closer to living your dreams.

1. What's The Dream?

The first step to achieving all your dreams is to identify what the dream is. You cannot expect to hit a target without setting up a concrete goal. Some who read these words will know exactly what they want. Others will have to stop and think about it for a minute or two. I encourage you to take some time to think about what you really want in life. This will help you set your objectives.

The following questions will help you set your goals. (Feel free to write in this book. It's yours.)

1) If the doctor told you that you only had six more months to live, what would you want to do in those six months?

_____
_____
_____

2) If you could achieve anything in the world, what would it be?

_____
_____
_____

3) What was the best feeling you ever had? What gave you the greatest sense of accomplishment?

_____
_____
_____

4) What's your legacy? What do you want to be remembered for?
_____
_____
_____

5) What might you say to your family and friends that you haven't been saying?
_____
_____
_____

6) What are your strengths and weaknesses?
_____
_____
_____

7) What event or cause would you be willing to stand up or die for to achieve?
_____
_____
_____

Asking these questions will give you an insight into what's most important in your life. Chances are, you already know what you want. It's just getting there that's the hard part! Maybe you want to become a doctor, lawyer, or fitness instructor. Maybe you want to quit your high-powered job and become a teacher or coach of a local team.

To be happy, you need a balance between work, family, personal, and spiritual. Yes, you need to carve out some personal time for yourself. No matter how busy you are, you can do that – a few moments a day to sit in your favorite chair and think, or a half hour to run outside.

You also need time for the spiritual side of you. I believe there is a major benefit to having a strong religious foundation, and to seeing your community of friends at your church or synagogue each week. It gives you a chance to surround yourself with good people who are undoubtedly doing good things.

I remember a sign I once saw in a London cathedral. It said: "Attempt Great Things for God." I never forgot that. Many people are already doing just that. George Brunstad who you met earlier, for instance, is raising money for desperately poor people in Haiti through his church.

George is still healthy, but at some point in our lives, we may hear the doctor tell us we only have another year to live. Then it might be too late to do what we really want to do. So, I think it's better to ask ourselves the question today – what is it we most want to do? Then we can start trying to achieve whatever it is … before it's too late.

2. Write It Down.

It really doesn't matter what your goal is. What matters is that you write it down. Writing down your goal will help you program your sub-conscious and give you something concrete to look at every day. It will help you concentrate on achieving your objective.

Having a goal written down becomes your target because you can't hit any target unless you know what it is. Even the world's greatest archer can't hit the bull's eye if he's blindfolded!

The very process of asking yourself these questions will give you an insight as to what is most important in your life. Try to balance your goals between work, family, personal and spiritual. Having a good balance for your goals will give you a good balance in life. But please, please: first you need some level of personal time for yourself. This could be a few moments a day to think about your life or to exercise to ensure you have good health to carry out what ever it is that you desire. You then will balance work and family time. Finally, a little spiritual time is always good as there are benefits to having a strong religious foundation. Peace of mind is not the least of them.

(Enter your goals. Go ahead – this is your book.)

Here are my goals:	Would like to Accomplish by Date:
1._____	_____
2._____	_____
3._____	_____
4._____	_____
5._____	_____
6._____	_____
7._____	_____
8._____	_____
9._____	_____
10._____	_____

3. Set A Deadline.

After you write down your goals, it's advantageous to set a deadline – a realistic one. A realistic date will enable you to chart your progress and not become discouraged.

If your goal is to earn more money, it may not be realistic to expect to triple your income in six months. But by acting toward that goal it may be possible for you to increase your earnings by 30 percent by then.

You may not be able to go from walking to running marathons in three months, but if you following some training guidelines, you may be able to do it in six months or a year.

Some goals may require a few years of

schooling. But the only way to achieve that goal might well be to take the first course and get going. Soon, the years will have zipped by and you will have earned that degree with pride.

Remember that whatever deadline you set, you'll need to build in extra time for unforeseen circumstances, the inevitable obstacles that pop-up like unwanted ads on your computer.

It's normal to encounter a few pop-up bumps. Just figure they'll be there. The more obstacles that you anticipate, the more you'll be mentally prepared. You'll feel like you're still on course, even while muddling through.

Given a believable goal and enough built-in time, you can achieve what you want. Try it.

4. The Plan.

Now it's time to write down a plan. Determine what kind of training, knowledge, or preparation will be required to achieve your goal. You may need the assistance of others, perhaps people or groups or organizations.

Is there a reason why these people should help you? Be sure you know what others will gain from your success. It may just be that your family members will gain a happier and more loving *you* because you feel really good inside. Your happiness will be contagious. The whole family will catch it!

All right, we're under way: list all the activities that you will need to accomplish your goals, and sort them out on a timeline of requirements.

Goal:	What I need to do:	Whom can I ask for help:

5. Action!

It is *not* enough to "want." You have to act. You need to put a plan into action. You need to do all the little things necessary to achieve your goal. My mother always said, "Break the job down into smaller jobs and tackle a little job first." So, break down your goal into smaller tasks. This will make it easier for you to get started. Start today and take action, one by one, on your smaller tasks. Soon you'll be rocketing toward your goal. Watch your confidence grow!

6. Daily Review.

My father used to say, "You have to write the business every day!" He meant you had to get out there, selling, every day or you will not meet the monthly or yearly goals. Accomplishing a dream is the same thing. You have to accomplish a piece of your dream plan every day. You can't make it up later. Later never comes!

You need to stick with your game plan and review it constantly. At the end of each day, take account of where you are on the escalator to your dreams. Figure out what is working and what isn't working for you. Before you go to sleep at night, ask yourself:

- What are my goals?
- Did I come closer to achieving my goals today?
- What can I do tomorrow?

Work toward your goal every day. If you feel you aren't making progress and are just stuck, unearth your road block ... then get by it. It's so easy to get sidetracked during the day with busywork that isn't helping you achieve your goal.

Here's a major test of your will-power: Try to focus on what is necessary to achieve your goal for the day and put off the other busy work until you complete your task.

It's okay to put off the busywork. It's not okay to put off your dreams.

7. Imagine Success!

See yourself as successful. Imagine what it will feel like when you finally achieve your dream. If you can *see* the success, then you will *achieve* the success. Repeat constantly this truth: You can achieve your goal and be happy!

Chapter Twenty
Desire – The Secret Ingredient To Achieving All That You Want.

Desire is the "fuel" you need to achieve your goals. If you have a fiery desire to accomplish a dream, then you can achieve it and no one will be able to stop you. Desire will help you overcome all the obstacles you face.

You may be a little short of money like the Rev. Dr. Gaston, but you'll find a way to earn it. You may not know everything you need to know to achieve your goal, but you'll find out like Dr. Gail Fredericks did. You may not have all the support you need from your family and friends at first, but when they see how passionate you are about your goal, they'll help.

With unblemished desire, all things are possible. As Ray Kroc put Calvin Coolidge's words in his autobiography, "Grinding it Out":

"Press on: Nothing in the world can take the place of persistence. Talent will not; nothing is more common than unsuccessful men with talent. Genius will not; unrewarded genius is almost a proverb. Education will not; the world is full of educated derelicts. Persistence and determination alone are omnipotent."

One of my favorite quotes comes from Donna de Varona's mother. Donna is a former Olympic gold-medal swimmer and one of the first champions of Title IX legislation to give girls equal sports opportunity.

"All things are possible," Mrs. De Varona said. "If you have the will, and you work hard, people along the way will help you. It will be hard, but you can do it."

The "Bandwagon Effect"!

I assure you: once you start plugging away at your dream, you'll gain supporters. They'll want to jump on your bandwagon like fans on a winning team.
This is a small chapter, but nonetheless critical because I believe desire is the single biggest motivator for achieving your goals. If you have a consistent, burning desire to achieve a particular goal for yourself, then you can achieve it. If your desired objective is in line with the spirit of who you really are and represents the values you genuinely have, the desire to achieve your goal will be very strong.

Desire will help you overcome all the obstacles you will face (and there probably will be many obstacles in front of you that you will have to deal with). You may be a little short of funds, a little short of knowledge, a little short on support, or a little short on physical ability.

None of that really matters if you have the desire to succeed. If you have the burning desire in your mind, then nothing or nobody will be able to stop you. If you are short of funds, you can build into your plan a way to make a few extra dollars or save a few dollars. If you don't currently possess the knowledge for your chosen task, you can begin studying today and plan enough time to gain the necessary knowledge. If you're out of shape to do what you want to do, today you can start walking; tomorrow you can run a few feet. The next day you'll cover a few blocks. Then a few miles...and then, the limits are within your grasp.

Certainly you may have a few nay-sayers along the way. *Do not* listen to negative comments. Just keep checking your goal and your plan to see if you are on target. If you have the desire to stay on target you will be on target and your desire will carry you to achieving your goal. The operative words: "I can."

Chapter Twenty-One
Exercise:
The Body Is The Carrier Of The Mind.

Although most of us have a healthy image of ourselves and believe that we are years younger than what we really are, we can't forget or overlook the "host" of our mind and spirit – the body.

Our bodies need to be kept in good working order. Otherwise the body could break down long before the mind does. I don't think you want to wake up one day and realize that your mind is working great, but your body needs a complete overhaul – it's exhausted and worn out. That not only would be more than frustrating; it absolutely could lead to depression.

The older you get, the more you need to be more concerned with a healthy body. Thus, good daily habits for healthy eating and exercise are a must. If you have good daily exercise habits, then you will be more alert and energetic during the day. Instead of becoming sleepy during the day, you'll be able to accomplish more of what you want to do.

People who intend to live longer need to take steps to protect their health and wellness. Make that *a lot of steps*, at least 30 minutes a day for at least three days a week. And don't stop because you've had another birthday. Stay active, regardless of age. One of your primary goals is to delay the onset of disease and disability and live independently as long as you possibly can.

A nasty statistic: currently, among people age 45 to 64, only 14 percent regularly engage in moderate physical activity for at least 30 minutes a day. Boomers recognize the importance of staying fit, and yet they too are falling short. Sad!.

While we can't avoid death, we can prolong our independence and avoid disease. Don't smoke ... eat right ... stay fit ... keep active and engaged.

OK?

Final Thoughts

I hope you found this book both helpful and inspirational. My goal was to jump start you towards thinking about your life long dreams and begin on the path to achieving all that you desire. By reading about people who have achieved their dreams later in life and the unifying principles that propelled them to their dreams, I hope that you can connect those principles to your own life.

Enough said.

Jeremy Goldstein

Reference Section

The following list of agencies and websites will provide you with useful information, resources and links to other informational sources.

AARP
601 E. Street, NW
Washington, DC 20049
Phone: 1-888-687-2277
www.aarp.org/careers-development/

With over 35 million members, AARP is the largest nonprofit membership organization dedicated to addressing the needs and interests of persons 50 and older. They have staffed offices in all 50 states, the District of Columbia, Puerto Rico and the U.S. Virgin Islands. This organization can help you answer many of your questions. The following are just a few:

WANT TO COME OUT OF RETIREMENT? AARP provides strategies for finding a second career after retirement. AARP also recommends career development and job search publications.

WANT TO FIND A NEW JOB? AARP offers insights on helping you find meaningful employment.

DO YOU WANT TO BE YOUR OWN BOSS? - AARP offers advice to consider before starting your own business.

WANT HELP HANDLING DIFFICULT INTERVIEW QUESTIONS? AARP helps you prepare for tough job interview questions.

WANT TO GO BACK TO SCHOOL? - AARP offers tips for adults planning to go back to school in order to change or enhance their careers.

DO YOU NEED HELP WRITING A RESUME? AARP can help you with the basics of writing a functional resume.

NOT SURE ABOUT YOUR CAPABILITIES? AARP can help you identify and evaluate which of your skills, abilities, and experiences are transferable to different jobs.

DO YOU THINK THAT IT IS TIME FOR A CAREER CHANGE? - AARP can help you decide if it is time

AARP (Best Employers for Workers Over 50)
AARP
601 E. Street NW
Washington, DC 20049
Phone: 888-687-2277
www.aarp.org/bestemployers

The AARP Best Employers for Workers Over 50 program honors employers who are ahead of the curve in recognizing the value of mature workers through their exemplary workplace policies and practices. A listing of the Best Employers can be found on the AARP web site by going directly to the address www.aarp.org/bestemployers.com.

Administration on Aging
Washington, DC 20201
Phone: 202 619-0724
www.aoa.gov

Administration on Aging site has information designed to help Americans live longer, healthier lives.

www.BoomerCareer.com
www.BoomerCareer.com/public/department10.cfm

Boomer Career.com is the publication for active Baby Boomers who want their careers to be vital components in fulfilled and challenging lives.

Experience Works, Inc
2200 Clarendon Blvd,
Suite 1000
Arlington, VA 22201
Phone:703-522-7272 or 866-397-9757
Fax: 703-522-0141

www.experienceworks.org/

Experience Works is a national, nonprofit organization that provides training and employment services for mature workers. Established in 1965 as Green Thumb, and renamed Experience Works in 2002, the organization reaches more than 125,000 mature individuals in all 50 states and Puerto Rico each year.

FirstGov.gov
www.FirstGov.gov

Whatever you want or need from the U.S. government, it's here on FirstGov.gov. You'll find a rich treasure of online information, services and resources. FirstGov.gov is the official U.S. gateway to all government information. There is a search capability on the site where you can search for various topics. A good place to start is by going directly to the address www.firstgov.gov/Topics/Seniors.shtml. This section will provide you with information regarding Health, Retirement, Job and a variety of other related topics.

Aetna InteliHealth
www.intelihealth.com

This website will provide you with Health and Lifestyle issues related to Seniors. On the home page you will find a Health Section. Click on "Seniors Health" for useful information for healthier lives.

International Longevity Center - USA
60 E. 86th Street
NY, NY 10028
Tel: 212-288-1468
Fax: 212-288-3132
info@ilcusa.org
www.ilcusa.org

The International Longevity Center-USA (ILC-USA) is a not-for-profit, nonpartisan research, policy and education organization whose mission is to help societies address the issues of population aging and longevity in positive and constructive ways and to highlight older people's productivity and contributions to their families and to society as a whole. This site provides "Publications" for various reports on aging. They also provide "Links" to several aging-related Web sites and services.

The National Council on the Aging
NCOA Headquarters
300 D Street, SW
Suite 801
Washington, D.C. 20024
Phone: 202-479-1200
Fax: 202-479-0735
E-mail: info@ncoa.org
www.maturityworks.org

Founded in 1950, The National Council on the Aging is a national network of organizations and individuals dedicated to improving the health and independence of older persons; increasing their continuing contributions to communities, society and future generations.

NIH Senior Health
Division of National Institutes of Health (NIH)
9000 Rockville Pike
Bethesda, Maryland 20892
www.nihseniorhealth.gov/exercise/toc.html

NIHSeniorHealth makes aging-related health information easily accessible for family members and friends seeking reliable, easy to understand online health information. This site was developed by the National Institute of Aging (NIA) and the National

Library of Medicine (NLM) both parts of the National Institute of Health (NIH). By going to the site index, you will find a section titled "Exercise for older Adults. This section discusses four types of exercise that are important for staying healthy including strength, balance, stretching and endurance exercises. This section also answers frequently asked questions and provides tips for charting progress and includes a video.

Seniors4Hire
C/o The Forward Group
7071 Warner Ave F466
Huntington Beach, CA 92647
Tel: (714) 848-0996
Fax: (714) 848-5445
Email: info@Seniors4Hire.org
www.Seniors4Hire.org

Seniors4Hire.org is a nationwide online Career Center for U.S. job seekers 50 and over to find job openings from businesses that value a diverse workforce and actively recruit and hire older workers, retirees and/or senior citizens.

Senior Job Bank
www.seniorjobbank.com/

The Senior Job Bank is a non-profit referral service - linking older workers (over 50), businesses and homeowners to create income opportunities for seniors wishing to re-enter or remain in the job marketplace in a part-time, temporary, occasional, flexible and even full-time basis. Senior Job Bank provides free links to sites that are relative to jobs for older workers.

Seniors Jobs.com
www.SeniorsJobs.Com

A Job Placement Service Matching Companies and Job Seekers Age 50 and Above. You can post your resume for free or search job postings from across America.

The Senior Job Bank
www.SeniorJobBank.org

Senior Job Bank provides free links to many sites that are relative to jobs for older workers. The Senior Job Bank encourages government, non-profit organizations and businesses to work together to help our seniors find 'meaningful' jobs.

Senior Journal.com
http://www.seniorjournal.com/seniorlinks.htm

This website provides information on Aging, Fitness, Nutrition, books and many other useful topics.

SeniorNet
121 Second St., 7th Floor
San Francisco, California 94105
TEL: 415-495-4990
FAX: 415-495-3999
www.seniornet.org

An award-winning site featuring book discussions, online tutorials and classes, discussions about computers, philosophy, health, arts and entertainment and free E-greetings. The organization supports over 240 Learning Centers throughout the U.S. and in other countries; publishes a quarterly newsletter and a variety of instructional materials; offers discounts on computer-related and other products and services; holds regional conferences and collaborates in research on older adults and technology.